LATIN AMERICA'S TURNAROUND

Since 1985 the International Center for Economic Growth, a nonprofit international policy institute, has contributed to economic growth and human development in developing and post-socialist countries by strengthening the capacity of indigenous research institutes to provide leadership in policy debates. To accomplish this the Center sponsors a wide range of programs—including research, publications, conferences, seminars, and special projects advising governments—through a network of over 250 correspondent institutes worldwide.

The Center is affiliated with the Institute for Contemporary Studies and is headquartered in Panama with the administrative office in San Francisco, California.

For further information, please contact the International Center for Economic Growth, 243 Kearny Street, San Francisco, California, 94108, USA. Phone (415) 981-5353; Fax (415) 986-4878.

ICEG Board of Overseers

LATIN AMERICA'S TURNAROUND

Privatization, Foreign Investment, and Growth

Edited by Paul H. Boeker

International Center for Economic Growth

Institute of the Americas

ICS PRESS
San Francisco, California

The Institute of the Americas is an independent, nonprofit institution devoted to finding effective responses to some of the major challenges facing the countries of the Western Hemisphere: consolidating democracy and market-oriented economic reforms, extending free trade, countering drug abuse and traffic, and halting environmental deterioration.

The Institute's projects support the trend toward economic integration and closer political cooperation in the hemisphere by helping to identify practical options for national policies and corporate strategies. Leaders in business, government, and academia from the United States, Canada, Latin America, and the Caribbean regularly participate in Institute projects, conferences, and publications.

In its second decade, the Institute of the Americas expects to extend its reach as the leading independent institution in the western United States focusing on the major economic, political, and social issues in the Americas.

Inquiries, book orders, and catalog requests should be addressed to ICS Press, 243 Kearny Street, San Francisco, California 94108, USA. Telephone: (415) 981-5353; fax: (415) 986-4878; book orders within the continental United States: **(800) 326-0263**.

Copyeditor: Deborah M. Styles

Indexer: Shirley Kessel

Cover designer: Irene Imfeld

Library of Congress Cataloging-in-Publication Data
Latin America's turnaround : privatization, foreign investment, and growth / edited by Paul H. Boeker.
    p. cm.
    Includes bibliographical references and index.
    ISBN 1-55815-247-4 (paper)
    1. Privatization—Latin America—Congresses. 2. Investments, Foreign—Latin America—Congresses. I. Boeker, Paul H.
    HD4010.5.L38   1993
    338.98—dc20   92-46168

CONTENTS

LIST OF TABLES AND FIGURES

LIST OF SELECTED ACRONYMS AND ABBREVIATIONS

ADS	American depository share
ANTEL	Administración Nacional de Telecomunicaciones (Uruguay)
BANAMEX	Banco Nacional de México
B/d	barrels per day
BHIF	Banco Hipotecario Internacional de Fomento (Chile)
BNDES	Banco Nacional de Desenvolvimento Econômico e Social (Brazil)
BOO	build-own-operate
BOOT	build-own-operate-transfer
Btus	British thermal units
CANTV	Compañía Anónima Nacional de Teléfonos de Venezuela (Venezuela)
CAP	Compañía de Acero del Pacífico (Chile)
CHILGENER	Compañía Chilena de Generación Eléctrica (Chile)
CHILMETRO	Compañía Chilena de Electricidad Metropolitana (Chile)

CHILQUINTA	Compañía Chilena de Electricidad de la Quinta Región (Chile)
CIE	Compagnie Ivoirienne d'Electricité (Côte d'Ivoire)
CNT	Comisión Nacional de Telecomunicaciones (Argentina)
CODELCO	Corporación del Cobre (Chile)
CORFO	Corporación de Fomento de la Producción (Chile)
CTC	Compañía de Teléfonos de Chile (Chile)
ECOM	Empresa Chilena de Computación e Informática (Chile)
EDELMAG	Empresa de Electricidad de Magallanes (Chile)
EECI	Energie Electrique de la Côte d'Ivoire (Côte d'Ivoire)
ELECDA	Empresa de Electricidad de Antofagasta (Chile)
ELIQSA	Empresa de Electricidad de Iquique (Chile)
EMELARI	Empresa de Electricidad de Arica (Chile)
ENAEX	Empresa Nacional de Explosivos (Chile)
ENAP	Empresa Nacional de Petróleo (Chile)
ENDESA	Empresa Nacional de Electricidad (Chile)
ENTEL	Empresa Nacional de Telecomunicaciones (Argentina)
ENTEL	Empresa Nacional de Telecomunicaciones (Chile)
FCC	Federal Communications Commission (United States)
FDI	foreign direct investment
GDP	gross domestic product
GNP	gross national product
GRIP	Guaranteed Recovery of Investment Principal (International Finance Corporation)
GW	gigawatt
IANSA	Industria Azucarera Nacional (Chile)
IDB	Inter-American Development Bank

kWh	kilowatt-hour
LAB	Lloyd Aéreo Boliviano (Bolivia)
LABCHILE	Laboratorios Chile (Chile)
LNG	liquefied natural gas
MIGA	Multilateral Investment Guarantee Agency
MW	megawatt
MYDFA	Multi-Year Deposit Facility Agreement
OECD	Organization for Economic Cooperation and Development
OLADE	Latin American Energy Association
OPEC	Organization of Petroleum Exporting Countries
OPIC	Overseas Private Investment Corporation
PDVSA	Petróleos de Venezuela, S.A. (Venezuela)
PEHUENCHE	Eléctrica Pehuenche (Chile)
PEMEX	Petróleos Mexicanos (Mexico)
PETROBRAS	Petróleo Brasileiro (Brazil)
PILMAIQUEN	Eléctrica Pilmaiquén (Chile)
SCT	Secretaría de Comunicaciones y Transportes (Mexico)
SEGBA	Servicios Eléctricos del Gran Buenos Aires (Argentina)
SISP	Société Internationale de Services Publiques (France)
SOE	State-owned enterprise
SOQUIMICH	Sociedad Química y Minera de Chile (Chile)
STET	Società Finanziaria Telefonica (Italy)
T&D	transmission and distribution
TELMEX	Teléfonos de México (Mexico)
USAID	U.S. Agency for International Development
USIMINAS	Usinas Siderúrgicas de Minas Gerais, S.A. (Brazil)
VASP	Viação Aérea São Paulo (Brazil)

VIASA	Venezolana Internacional de Aviación, S.A. (Venezuela)
YPF	Yacimientos Petrolíferos Fiscales (Argentina)
YPFB	Yacimientos Petrolíferos Fiscales Bolivianos (Bolivia)

PREFACE

When the decade of the 1980s opened, the state was the engine of economic growth in Latin America. From the 1930s through the 1970s, Latin American economies were characterized by ever-greater state control. Governments from Mexico to Argentina nationalized what they considered "strategic" industries. New state-owned enterprises burgeoned. Direct foreign investment was excluded, to be replaced by state borrowing from abroad.

After the recession and debt crisis of the early 1980s forced a rethinking of economic strategy in Latin America, however, a new generation of leaders came to power, determined to set their economic houses in order. Carlos Salinas de Gortari in Mexico, Carlos Menem in Argentina, and others, following the early example of Chile, aimed to turn the productive sector of the economy back over to the private sector. Because local investors in many Latin American countries were short on capital, both for purchasing these enterprises and for making necessary new investments in some industries, governments in the late 1980s began looking to foreign investors.

Latin America's Turnaround: Privatization, Foreign Investment, and Growth documents and analyzes this remarkable shift in economic thinking. It presents the findings of the Second International Conference on Privatization in Latin America, sponsored by the Institute of the Americas and held in April 1991. The Institute gathered policy makers, academics, journalists, and businesspeople to look at this two-pronged strategy of privatizing state enterprises and attracting foreign investment. The participants assess the progress of privatization and foreign investment in individual countries and economic sectors, pointing out the opportunities available and the challenges to be met. In the telecommunications industry, for instance, the task for Latin American countries is to develop regulatory arrangements that will both encourage the extension of basic telephone service and stimulate the competition needed to produce more sophisticated telecommunications services. For the electric power sector, privatization may be the only way of raising efficiency and attracting enough capital to meet the huge need for new investment in the sector.

The associated trends toward a smaller state role in the economy and a dynamic private sector that includes foreign investors hold great promise for Latin America. These developments could lead not only to greater prosperity, but also to improved services from government, which will be better able to carry out its basic commitments—related to education, public health, and roads, for example—without the financial burden of debt-laden state enterprises. *Latin America's Turnaround*, copublished by the International Center for Economic Growth and the Institute of the Americas, offers valuable insights into this exciting period and will be useful to policy makers not only in the Western Hemisphere but also in other developing regions of the world.

Nicolás Ardito-Barletta
General Director
International Center for Economic Growth

Panama City, Panama
March 1993

Acknowledgments

This book and the project from which it evolved were made possible by support from the following institutions: the Pew Charitable Trusts; the Andrew W. Mellon Foundation; the United States Trade and Development Program; the United States Agency for International Development, Office of Energy, Private Sector Energy Development Program; the California Energy Commission; the University of California, San Diego, Graduate School of International Relations and Pacific Studies; Bell Atlantic International, Inc.; and Solar Turbines, Inc.

Jason Hafemeister provided valuable research assistance to the editor. Gail Sevrens contributed both copyediting and research assistance. Jeff Carmel also provided editorial support.

LATIN AMERICA'S TURNAROUND

PART ONE

FOREIGN INVESTMENT IN LATIN AMERICA'S PRIVATIZATION

Latin America's Economic Opening and the Rediscovery of Foreign Investment

Over the past thirty years Latin America's approach to foreign investment has come full circle, along with its approach to economic growth. The foreign investor, once nationalized and almost declared obsolete, has become a critical player in Latin America's drive for modernization and renewed growth. And the debt-laden state enterprise, once portrayed as the Latin substitute for foreign equity investment, is being privatized virtually everywhere in Latin America. The most graphic reflection of Latin America's new approach to growth is the point at which foreign investment and privatization come together: Latin America's quest to get foreign buyers for the large number of former state enterprises it plans to sell—hundreds of companies, including many of the region's largest, with a total value that could reach US$100 billion in assets before the 1990s are over.

The change is so dramatic and complete that one must ask: will it last? The answer to that question is by and large a positive one. Privatization and openness to foreign investment are fundamental parts of Latin America's new approach to economic growth, an approach that is bringing the region out of the stagnation in which the turgid inflexibilities of state capitalism left it mired. The new approach has also thrived on Latin America's disillusionment with big government and on the modern political philosophy of the region's leadership and people.

Full Circle to State Capitalism and Back

A look at the complete circle Latin America has made reveals how fundamental is Latin America's rejection of its own expansive, wasteful version of state capitalism. In the 1960s and early 1970s the doctrine that the state needed to control "strategic industries" spawned a wave of nationalizations of natural resource companies as well as many basic industries: electric power companies, communications companies, shipping and transportation firms—even manufacturing industries. Many of these had long been wholly or partially owned by foreign investors. As a result, many U.S. companies lost significant assets in Latin America to nationalizations, including such long-standing firms in Latin America as American and Foreign Power, Standard Oil, International Telephone & Telegraph, GTE, and W. R. Grace, among others.

In the 1970s Latin American planners and bureaucrats continually extended their concept of "strategic industries" and of the role of the state as the producer of economic growth. Strategic industries came to include anything up to and including fish meal in Peru, trucking in Mexico, and zippers in Brazil. Countries that could afford it, such as Mexico and Brazil, launched an increasing number of state-owned enterprises to fulfill each perceived new opportunity for faster national development. During the oil boom this trend was accelerated by easy money, as Latin America's oil-producing countries came into new wealth and the others found foreign commercial banks flush with oil producers' deposits to lend to state enterprises in the region.

In this heady but fleeting environment, state planners and heads of state enterprises developed a rationale for their role that virtually cast the state enterprise and its ability to borrow abroad as the modern replacement for foreign direct investment. The argument was, in short, that Latin economies could get the money from bankers without giving foreign firms any right to future profits or direct influence in enterprise decisions. The nationalistic tone of this argument also helped to rationalize high import protection, which many state enterprises needed, and to present concentration on the domestic market as a virtue, rather than a limitation arising from these enterprises' inability to compete in the international market. At the same time many foreign investors lost interest in Latin America as rising costs in its protected domestic markets made production for export in Latin America unprofitable.

Under this extensive concept of the state's responsibility for the productive economy, it was an easy step to assume that any important private firm that became insolvent should be brought into the public sector, rather than be allowed to fail. As Brazil's Fernando Collor de Mello put it:

The state has always been a large hospital. When a private company experienced difficulties, it had a line of credit here or there to help it continue operations. The most superficial analysis would have shown that [the] company was not able to survive. When the money was imprudently lent by the state [and] that company again had difficulties, the state took it over.[1]

In the judgment of Jacques Rogozinski, director of Mexico's Office of Privatization, 50 percent of Mexico's state-owned enterprises were failing at the time of acquisition, and many should have been liquidated, rather than taken over in the mistaken assumption that a takeover was an effective way to save jobs.[2]

Indeed, the state had in many cases guaranteed the foreign borrowing that overextended many of Latin America's thinly capitalized private firms in the 1970s. Thus, when the international financial crisis of 1982–1983 struck, Latin American governments found themselves less than enthusiastic owners of another wave of enterprises. The government of Venezuela, for example, suddenly found itself massively involved in the hotel business, and even General Augusto Pinochet's Chile became the new owner of hundreds of banks, financial services, and other firms it did not want.

By the 1970s a region that had never seen itself as socialist found itself with an enormous public sector, consisting of enterprises producing everything from steel to matches. Mexico had more than 1,000 state-owned enterprises by the early 1970s; Chile, 650; Venezuela, 400; and Brazil, 200. In Brazil these state-owned enterprises accounted for over half of gross national product (GNP), and in Chile close to half of GNP. The state had become, like the giant of *Gulliver's Travels*, huge but immobilized, without power in its limbs and unable to perform its most essential functions. As Fernando Collor de Mello saw it:

The state is a giant. It is inefficient, and it is corrupt. The state controls 75 percent of the Brazilian economy, yet despite being a gigantic apparatus it is unable to pay dignified salaries, it is unable to supply enough chalk for the teachers in the schools, it is unable to distribute Mercurochrome and gauze to health posts to heal children who fall from their bicycles or who hurt themselves while playing ball on the street. Despite being gigantic, the state is inefficient.[3]

President Carlos Menem in Argentina paints the same picture:

Permanent interventionism and, worst of all, a penniless administration cannot meet the needs of the people and cannot finance growth, because such a gargantuan state can only absorb the wealth of people and prevent the country from growing despite the huge national economic potential.[4]

The foreign debt crisis, which quickly spread to most of Latin America after the Mexican payments crisis of 1982, brought an abrupt end to both

Latin America's economic growth and the house of cards that had held it up—a grotesquely overgrown state capitalism living on borrowed money and postponed reform.

As Latin leaders in the 1980s sorted through the wreckage of their collapsed economic houses, they discovered that the state enterprises and their mounting debts had brought the roof down. "The weight of the state became unbearable for society as a whole," in Collor de Mello's words.[5]

Latin America's leaders awoke to find that a panoply of state enterprises, only loosely under their control, had borrowed heavily, incurring debt that their governments could no longer pay. These enterprises were earning neither the local currency nor the foreign exchange to meet their obligations. By the early 1980s half of Latin America's public sector deficits were accounted for by state enterprises, as compared with 25 percent ten years earlier. The combined debt of state enterprises in Latin America's largest economies in 1983 was staggering: US$37.6 billion in Argentina, US$53.3 billion in Brazil, and US$50.6 billion in Mexico. Far from achieving financial independence for Latin American economies, the state enterprises had both put the national governments in hock to foreign commercial bankers and fueled debilitating domestic inflation through the continuous red ink flowing to cover their operating deficits and constant capital infusions.

In their determination to stop the hemorrhage of national resources into the deficits of the state enterprises, a new set of Latin American leaders stumbled briefly through campaigns to rationalize the operations of these enterprises through new management, higher product prices, and controls on payroll and new borrowing. As Ravi Ramamurti points out in chapter 3, "Privatization as a Remedy for State-owned Enterprises," such efforts to reform state enterprises had done little to improve their financial performance over an extended period. The result was no different in the 1980s. By the mid-1980s the most aggressive political leaders had leaped to more radical solutions: liquidation and privatization—the sale of the public sector's enterprises to private investors.

At first the privatization of state enterprises was not seen as one in which foreign private investors were to play a significant part. Chile, the pioneer in Latin America's rolling wave of privatizations, launched its first rounds of such sales in the mid-1970s in a way that overwhelmingly targeted domestic investors, even lending them the money to buy companies they could not really afford. A few countries did tentatively experiment with debt-equity swaps, offering foreigners who would buy some of the government's heavily discounted debt in secondary markets the opportunity to exchange it for a higher nominal value of shares in certain national companies.

Early experiments with debt-equity swaps may have appeared to bring the role of foreign direct investment full circle, since they replaced some foreign loans to state enterprises with foreign equity ownership. But the actual purpose of these early operations was directed more at debt reduction than at attracting foreign direct investment. Nevertheless, by 1991 these debt-equity swaps had become significant instruments for bringing foreign investment back into Latin American economies as well. Chile had by 1991 carried out over US$3.5 billion of such debt-equity conversions, and Argentina converted over US$7 billion of its debt with two large privatizations, the sales of Aerolíneas Argentinas, the national airline, and of ENTEL, the state telephone company.

Privatization brought Latin America's approach to foreign direct investment full circle only as Latin objectives for privatization expanded beyond crash programs of budget cutting to structural reform programs aimed at more efficient economies. This expansion of objectives occurred as part of a broader transformation in Latin America's approach to economic growth in general.

Throughout the 1980s virtually all of Latin America rejected the entire economic approach that included a leading role for state enterprises. Under the new approach, economies were deregulated and opened to international competition, and the government's intervention in the productive sector was scaled back to nurture more competitive, and less inflationary, economies. In chapter 2, "The Accelerating Pace of Privatization in Latin America," several experts describe the status of privatization in many of these countries. And as Latin American economies implemented these reforms, they fulfilled many of the requirements for successful foreign participation in their privatizations, requirements that are elaborated by Edgar C. Harrell in chapter 4, "Privatization Requirements of Foreign Investors."

As bright government economists and savvy political leaders took a sharper look at the role of privatization in this longer-term transformation, they found a new set of objectives, based on increasing efficiency, acquiring high-quality technology, producing better services to support competitive economies, and securing the huge amounts of investment needed to capitalize adequately some of their largest enterprises.

As frequently happens in democratic societies, the public was ahead of political leadership in receiving this revelation. Public opinion polls in Latin American countries have consistently shown strong popular support for privatization. In Argentina and Peru, 80 percent of the people polled have favored privatization, while 58 percent in Chile have supported it. In their responses to the polls, the people stressed not their desire to have their countries borrow less abroad or even to reduce public sector deficits, but rather the need for better and more efficient services than those provided by the state enterprises.

The public's reaction to privatization focused on phones that did not work or took years to get installed; on continual power outages; and on public transportation that ran erratically, when not on strike. The Argentines' view of state enterprises was dominated not by economic philosophy but by poor services: three tries required to make a local phone call connection; line failures at twelve times the international average; up to forty days for phone repair; and four years' wait for installation of a new phone line. A frustrated public endured poor services and witnessed the ensuing drag on the efficiency of the entire economy. The appeal to the public was that private companies, driven by profit incentives, would be more responsive to consumer demands and more likely to improve products and services.

As governments expanded their focus on privatization as a key part of the transformation to more efficient economies, the requirements for successful privatization expanded beyond stopping the deficits and getting a good price for the treasury to such factors as introducing real competition in the privatized industry and attracting investors with adequate capital to modernize and improve products and services and with access to the best technology. The logic was apparent that including foreign investors in the competition to purchase privatizing enterprises increased the prospects of meeting all of these requirements. More bidders meant better value for the treasury; more participants in the privatized industry meant greater competition; foreign investors, as consortium partners, increased the capital base of the owners of the privatized enterprise; major international companies as investors meant direct access to the best technology available, since these were the companies that owned such technology.

The New Quest for Foreign Investors in Privatized Companies and Industries

In the late 1980s, therefore, Latin America's governments launched a quest to attract foreign direct investors to privatizing companies and industries. In its third and fourth round of privatizations, beginning in the mid-1980s, Chile adopted tax and foreign exchange incentives to attract foreign investor participation in its continuing privatizations, as Juan Foxley Rioseco describes in chapter 6, "Financial Incentives for Investment in Chile's Privatization." One of the reasons for this was Chile's own experience in the largely failed early privatizations in the mid-1970s. Most of these hastily privatized companies went bankrupt in the severe recession of 1982–1983. As Edgar C. Harrell points out in chapter 4, privatized firms that had substantial foreign participation tended to survive the shock of this deep recession because they were better capitalized, while most of their domestic counterparts failed.

By the end of the 1980s the governments of Mexico, Chile, Argentina, and Venezuela were among those trying to privatize some of their countries' largest firms, such as their respective telephone companies. In the case of these huge privatizations the need for foreign capital participation and sophisticated technology was clear. And the public's demand for better services was reflected in extensive requirements for improved services to which successful bidders for the privatized company had to commit, requirements that went far beyond what the state telecommunications companies had planned. As Ben A. Petrazzini describes in chapter 5, "Foreign Direct Investment in Latin America's Privatization," the role of foreign investors in Latin America's privatizations grew steadily over the 1980s, and by 1990 premier international companies were making investments of hundreds of millions of dollars, and in some cases over US$1 billion, in Latin privatizations.

Domestic capital shortage is now a major factor moving Latin American governments to look to privatize sectors and industries, rather than just the existing companies in them. Given the inadequacy of domestic savings, the objective has become to attract foreign capital to carry out the new investment required in capital-intensive sectors, electric power, telecommunications, transportation, water supply, and sewerage, and even the last bastion of the doctrine of the "strategic industry," petroleum and natural gas.

As Fernando Collor de Mello starkly put it: "[Why] privatization of new investments in the electricity, transportation, and communications areas? Because Brazil will have to invest nearly $30 billion in the electricity area alone in the next four years so that the country will not collapse due to lack of energy. . . . we do not have the internal savings to meet the demand for these investments."[6]

The Opportunity of the Century

The final four chapters of this book analyze the major sectors that Latin American countries are privatizing and opening to new foreign private investment. These sectors are the largest and most capital intensive in modern economies: telecommunications, electric power, petroleum and natural gas, and tourism and transportation. In all of them, Latin American countries are looking for significant foreign investment to meet their needs for capital, technology, and improved products and services. The countries that can increasingly attract such investment are those that had earlier embarked on comprehensive economic reforms. They now present even foreign investors jaded by earlier disappointments with a much more stable economic environment than they had faced in the unstable 1970s and the stagnant first half of the 1980s.

The combination of the quest for foreign investment in privatized industries and more stable and open economies has suddenly created the largest opportunity ever for foreign investors to buy into Latin America's economies—over US$100 billion in new capital for privatized industries that Latin America seeks to attract during the 1990s from investors abroad.

In chapter 7, "Privatization as an Objective: Telecommunications and Regulatory Reform," Mark S. Fowler and Aileen Amarandos Pisciotta point out that the major challenge for Latin America's telecommunications industry is still ahead. Basic telecommunications services have penetrated only about 10 percent of Latin America's market, compared with well over 90 percent penetration in the United States. The challenge, therefore, is to develop a regulatory structure that both propels extension of basic telephone service and encourages the competition needed to meet modern business and consumer demands for more sophisticated telecommunications services. Many foreign companies are moving to take advantage of the proliferating opportunities in Latin America's telecommunications industry for these so-called value-added services—such as fax, cellular, and private communications networks—in the more competitive environment now opening up.

In chapter 8, "Private Participation in the Electric Power Sector," James B. Sullivan cites Latin America's need for US$155 billion in new capital in the 1990s for the power sector alone. Furthermore, the region will need to achieve significantly increased system efficiency if even this huge amount of capital is to be adequate to deliver the power required by the market. Private participation provides a potential solution to both these problems, capital shortage and system inefficiency. The techniques likely to be employed include independent generating plants, industrial cogenerating and self-generating, privatization of electricity production through ownership and leasing, and privatization of electricity provision through management contracting.

In chapter 9, "Oil and Natural Gas Privatization," Kim Fuad recounts the careful process by which tens of billions of dollars of foreign private investment are being attracted, both by outright privatizations, as in the case of Argentina's national oil company, and by various forms of joint ventures with the major national oil companies, led by Petróleos de Venezuela, S.A. (PDVSA). The growing participation of foreign private investors in Latin America's oil and gas industry reflects a significant turn away from the resource nationalism that swept Latin American countries in the 1960s and 1970s.

Tourism and air transportation together constitute the largest industry of many countries in Latin America and the Caribbean. This industry is covered by David L. Edgell, Sr., and Wanda Barquin in chapter 10, "Privatization of Tourism and Air Transportation." Mexico and Jamaica have led the way in privatizations. Mexico has privatized its major airlines and over twenty hotels; Jamaica has sold over US$100 million worth of hotels to Jamaican and foreign investors. Other Latin American countries are following, since privatization appears to offer the best prospects for meeting the demands of tourists for higher quality services.

The Last Promise for Privatization

The latest generation of Latin America's political leadership has taken the objectives and promise of privatization one step farther into the bold new world of economic and political reform in Latin America. Brash young leaders such as Carlos Salinas de Gortari in Mexico have presented the ambitious thesis that a leaner state can be a more just state. They have argued, correctly, that the huge consumption of the state's resources and energies in state capitalism left too little for state social programs: in effect, that the state's core functions of education, public health, roads, and welfare were sapped of funds because the state was using and losing all its resources in trying to produce goods and services that the private sector could produce better. But this sound neo-liberal criticism of the past is also a promise for the future, a new commitment by which leaders have set themselves up to be judged.

Carlos Salinas said it most eloquently, but all too plainly, in the first annual report of his government:

> The reality is that in Mexico a larger state has resulted in less capacity to respond to the social demands of our fellow citizens and, in the end, greater weakness of the state itself. As the public sector's productive activities grew, its attention to potable water supply, health, rural investment and food supply, housing, the environment, and justice decreased. The size of the state was growing while the well-being of the people was deteriorating. . . . As the facts show, the state concerned itself more with administering its properties than with meeting pressing social needs. . . . the focal point of the state reform is to reach decisions that benefit the people, to resolve the dilemma between property to be managed or justice to be dispensed, between a more proprietary state or a more just state.[7]

The fulfillment of this promise, of course, depends not so much on the privatized enterprises producing good services and paying increased tax revenues to the treasury, which is already happening. The fulfillment of the promise of a more just state depends on what the treasury does with the revenues, which is a question for the state, not the privatized enterprises. To this extent, the final consolidation of political support for Latin America's economic reforms will be achieved when its leaders fulfill their promise of better social services from a leaner state.

In the marketplace, Latin America's economic reform and privatization programs now appear irreversible. Increasing foreign participation in the region's extensive privatizations has become a touchstone of success for both these drives. It has also become the ultimate measure of Latin America's opening to the world market. In this new environment Latin America's ambitious quest to attract extensive foreign capital and technology is the widest opportunity ever presented to foreign investors in Latin America.

Notes

1. Television interview on Rede Globo, March 19, 1990; quoted in *Foreign Broadcast Information Service* (*FBIS*), March 21, 1990, p. 33.

2. Presentation to the Institute of the Americas' Second International Conference on Privatization, University of California, San Diego, La Jolla, California, April 14–16, 1991.

3. Debate with presidential candidate Lula, Rede Globo, December 3, 1989; quoted in *FBIS*, December 6, 1989, p. 27.

4. Speech on December 18, 1989, Buenos Aires Domestic Service; quoted in *FBIS*, December 19, 1989, p. 38.

5. Television interview on Rede Globo, March 19, 1990; quoted in *FBIS*, March 21, 1990, p. 33.

6. Ibid., p. 36.

7. October 1989 State of the Union Address, from William Glade, ed., *Privatization of Public Enterprises in Latin America* (San Francisco: ICS Press, 1991), p. 17.

The Accelerating Pace of Privatization in Latin America

An Overview

WILLIAM A. ORME, JR.

Once started, the privatization bandwagon careered across the Americas with stunning alacrity. In a region once defined by zealous statism, virtually everything in government hands seems suddenly to be up for sale. And there is little doubt that Latin American governments are genuinely committed to privatization.

The young technocrats who staff finance ministries from Buenos Aires to Mexico City reveal striking similarities in their analyses and aims. They live in a subculture shaped by pragmatism, not theology, and they see the contrast between Eastern Europe and East Asia as a clear object lesson in development economics. The new generation of politicians to whom these technicians report also tend to be practical people: they want to know simply what works and what does not, even when it contradicts their own parties' creeds.

The favored buzzword of this new breed of reformers is "irreversible." Economic change does indeed appear to be so sweeping and profound that is hard to imagine a return to nationalization and import substitution.

The biggest immediate problem is the marketplace itself. The global privatization craze has created a buyer's market in airlines, steel mills, and other budget-bleeding properties. To sell at an attractive price is getting harder all the time: witness the 1991 collapse of Puerto Rico's effort to sell a telecommunications monopoly—and this in a dollar economy free of foreign bank debt and hyperinflation.

Competition from sellers within and beyond the region is forcing Latin America to confront the basic paradox of privatization: inefficient businesses that drain the treasury attract few bidders, while well-managed enterprises that pump in capital are the easiest to divest.

Some investors say the most attractive properties in the most attractive economies have already been sold. Businesses that welcome a chance to buy a bank or petrochemical plant in stable, fast-growing Mexico will spurn similar opportunities—whatever the price—in turbulent Peru. While Mexican President Carlos Salinas de Gortari's administration has the economic luxury of demanding better bids, Alberto Fujimori's government in Peru may feel obligated to accept the first serious offer, thus reinforcing the suspicions of Peruvian critics who see privatization as a fire-sale giveaway. Peru has discovered, as have other countries, that a thorough privatization campaign can be carried out only in the exacting context of real deregulation and noninflationary growth.

Chile

Some hard-nosed business observers look back at the cyclical swings of Latin American politics and question whether privatization and its attendant reforms could in fact be reversed in a different ideological climate. Chile, as the trailblazer, offers some useful lessons. Many if not most Latin American leaders were repelled by the dictatorial taint of General Augusto Pinochet's free-market reforms. But even hostile observers soon concluded that the sale of state companies was the essential ingredient of Chile's undeniably successful recipe for growth. Privatization eliminated the budget deficit—thus checking inflation and stabilizing the currency—while raising funds for social spending. Debt swap provisions turned foreign creditors into investors. The "people's capitalism" strategy—making savvy stockholders out of employees and ordinary citizens—helped to decentralize the economy and invigorate the moribund securities market.

More important, the Chilean experiment was an unquestionable political success. In its 1989 campaign pledges not to repeal privatization, the center-left opposition was reflecting its own reading of public sentiment, and astute office seekers elsewhere in Latin America took careful note. The key, however, was Chile's overall macroeconomic success: the Pinochet team understood that if it didn't pull the economy out of recession, a backlash was inevitable.

In retrospect, Chile was doubly fortunate in going first. Its telephone and power companies were among the few such business opportunities in the world at the time, and they fetched strong bids from solid investors. The conversion to an export model came at a time when the United States was setting import records and Chile had few regional competitors. In the early stages of the debt crisis, bankers were more eager to cooperate with a by-the-books borrower—especially one at least temporarily exempt from the constraints and uncertainties of democracy.

Mexico

Mexico was the next big economy to clamber aboard. It was also fortunate that it began to move early. In its eagerness to assuage creditors, the De la Madrid regime at first exaggerated its privatization progress: while it was true as claimed that Mexico eliminated "hundreds of state entities" in the mid-1980s, most were dysfunctional agencies or workshops that could be decreed painlessly out of existence. The hyperbole helped in the long run, though. By ballyhooing its modest initial achievements, the government inured the public to an endless roll call of "divested, merged, or liquidated" enterprises. By the time meaningful sales began late in the decade—the airlines, the phone company, copper conglomerates—the left-wing opposition found it hard to arouse much outrage. Now banks that were expropriated amid populist ceremony just a decade ago are being divested with little fear of electoral reprisal.

Argentina

Argentina, unlike Mexico, was saddled with a woeful debtor's record and the benign neglect of G-7 treasuries, limiting its appeal to investors. Bids were few. In one of the great ironies of Latin America's privatization drive, the national airline and half the phone company were "privatized" into the hands of state monopolies from Spain. But the debt impasse was broken—and, along with it, a deep-rooted nationalist taboo against foreign investment in public services.

Brazil

Brazil's belated rapprochement with its creditors is now getting Latin America's biggest privatization program back on track, despite the collapse of the Collor presidency and the absence of any clear national consensus on economic policy. As in Argentina, the immediate impetus was the need to clear up interest arrears. When banks conclude a reduction-and-restructuring deal for the US$50 billion commercial foreign debt, they will receive ten-year bonds in payment for US$7 billion in past-due interest—bonds they can then swap for shares in privatized companies.

Foreign investors may be loathe to acquire interests in Brazil's giant state-owned steel mills and petrochemical complexes at a time of global recession and excess capacity. For public enterprises, however, Brazilian heavy industries enjoy a reputation for technological competitiveness well above the Latin American norm. One encouraging factor is the propensity of Brazilians to invest in their own economy, adversity and inflation notwithstanding. The successful sale of Viação Aérea São Paulo (VASP) airline to trucking magnate Wagner Canhedo could bode well for future privatization efforts.

Other countries

The privatization outlook is murkier for the poorer, smaller economies—such as those of Honduras, Ecuador, the Dominican Republic, and Paraguay—that offer neither the stability nor the sheer scale that most investors require. At the other end of the economic spectrum, exemplified by richly endowed Venezuela, the prospects appear equally uncertain. Without a palpable sense of emergency, the commitment to reform can quickly abate.

Politics and privatization

Still privatization seems likely to prevail in most Latin American econ-omies, and not because of some sudden Saulesque conversion to the gospel of Adam Smith. Privatization has advanced as far as it has in Latin America because there are few alternatives—and because it is politically prudent. As politicians from Patagonia to the Rio Grande have discovered to their chagrin, the legacy of expropriation exposes incumbents to grave political risks. If the phone doesn't work, if a flight is canceled, if coffee in the market is stale and consumer appliances are shoddy and overpriced, the fault ultimately lies with the president, or at least with the president's party.

Critics note that in no Latin American country has a wholesale priva-tization effort yet been endorsed by voters. Messrs. Menem, Collor de Mello, Pérez, and Fujimori ran ambiguously populist campaigns that promised macroeconomic growth, not public sector downsizing. Carlos Salinas was more forthright about his intentions, yet his campaign stressed what the state planned to keep (oil, primarily) more than what it planned to sell (banks, airlines, steel mills, the phone company). And Mr. Salinas barely managed a plurality in the most disastrous setback Mexico's ruling party had experienced in its sixty years in power.

By contrast, Mario Vargas Llosa in Peru and Hernán Buchi in Chile pledged radical deregulation, divestiture, and fealty to the law of the marketplace. They were the only overtly neo-Thatcherite presidential candidates Latin America had ever seen, and both were soundly trounced.

More important, perhaps, is that nobody is moving in the opposite direction. Once installed in office, politicians throughout the region have been able to sell state companies with little resistance. State companies are seen as costly sinecures for unqualified cronies, providing abysmal service and vast opportunities for graft. Few genuinely regret their demise. Significantly, there is no evidence that any Latin American opposition bloc believes it can make electoral gains by proposing the return of divested companies to the public sector fold.

Instead, the mechanics of privatization has come under intense criticism. Complaints, many justifiable, have centered on the specific terms of sales, including bidding procedures, treatment of workers' contracts and pensions, the viability of consortiums of private buyers, and special concessions to foreign creditors. In too many cases privatization has led to a dangerous reconcentration of private economic power (in one example, a single Mexican industrialist now owns 95 percent of his country's newly privatized copper reserves).

But the focus of debate has been the pace, price, and methodology of privatization, rather than privatization itself. In most cases, governments have proceeded with care and stealth. Sales policies usually conform to an implicit national consensus on which properties are essential to the state and which are not. Venezuela is privatizing offshore natural gas deposits to underwrite massive development costs, but it would not consider the sale of onshore, easily exploited, commercially viable crude reserves. Neither would Mexico. The classic example is Chile's state copper company, CODELCO, the inheritor of mines nationalized by the Frei and Allende regimes, which the Pinochet government never offered to the market (indeed, the Chilean military awarded itself a direct cut of CODELCO's revenues).

Even enthusiasts couch their support for privatization with concerns about reconcentrated wealth and the sale of undervalued assets during a global recession. Multilateral insistence on rapid privatization by all may face the same problem as the old International Monetary Fund advocacy of fat simultaneous trade surpluses for all third world debtors. Not everybody can sell at once.

Ultimately, though, the options are limited. For Latin America's pragmatic new breed of economic managers, privatization's continuing appeal calls to mind the Churchillean dictum about democracy: it is the worst strategy for economic revival, except for all the rest.

Argentina

PABLO L. GERCHUNOFF

In the space of a few months Argentina's economy underwent a transformation far more rapid and extensive than the massive privatization program carried out by Margaret Thatcher in the United Kingdom in the early 1980s. Between the latter half of 1990 and early 1991, the government of Carlos Menem privatized Argentina's state telephone company (ENTEL); its national airline, Aerolíneas Argentinas; national highway maintenance services; a significant amount of its petroleum reserves; its stake in several petrochemical firms; and two television channels. Other important privatizations are under way for the country's gas and electric utilities; the national water and sewage company; all of the petrochemical and iron and steel companies; the entire complex of firms linked to the military; and at least a part of Yacimientos Petrolíferos Fiscales (YPF), the national petroleum company. By 1993 the Argentine government intends to have removed itself from most financial services and, with the exception of a small remaining participation in the hydrocarbon sector, all production activities.

Broad support exists in Argentina for this large-scale sell-off of state enterprises, for two reasons. First, Argentina's state enterprises have been notoriously inefficient and poorly managed, victims, analysts say, of political instability, increased influence-peddling by government contractors and unions, and the lack of administrative independence. Second, the government will no longer be obligated to finance the investments of state enterprises. Since the beginning of the foreign debt crisis the public sector has been forced to slash capital expenditures. The cuts in spending have caused further deterioration in public services.

Like Argentina's huge nationalization programs of the 1940s, the government's privatization policies of the 1990s seem to be pursuing multiple objectives: improving the quality of services; increasing private financing of investments; limiting the power of unions and big business; reducing the foreign debt by converting much of it to shares in privatized companies, thus alleviating pressure on the balance of payments; and obtaining additional liquidity for the public sector in an effort to stabilize the economy.

During the first phase of the Argentine privatizations, priority was given to those objectives linked to macroeconomic stabilization. Argentina had just passed through two periods of hyperinflation, the Treasury's situation was critical, and there was increasing pressure from foreign creditors trying to collect debt payments that were in arrears (the country had just ended an eighteen-month self-declared moratorium on debt payments).

As a consequence these early privatizations aimed to reestablish the state's cash flow and to put the foreign accounts in order. The sale of petroleum reserves—about US$1 billion—helped to refill the country's nearly empty coffers; the sales of ENTEL and Aerolíneas Argentinas were carried out almost wholly through a scheme for converting the government's own debt into private equity. Under this scheme the country was able to wipe out some US$7 billion of its own debt, almost 20 percent of its total debt to the commercial banks. In effect the foreign investors were allowed to buy deeply discounted Argentine government debt abroad and to apply it at face value to their required investment in ENTEL and the airline.

Privatization in Argentina, as an instrument of internal and external financial policy, has entailed some costs. In the rush to complete the sale of companies and shares, most public services were transferred without an adequate regulatory environment to protect consumers. At the same time rates charged for these services were increased sharply prior to the privatizations in an effort to facilitate the financing of the investments through retained earnings of the privatized enterprises.

The privatizations were carried out in an economy without a capital market, so there was no process of broad diffusion of ownership, as in the United Kingdom. Instead, these early privatizations created closely held companies, with ownership concentrated in a few hands and with the majority of shares held by foreign firms. The mechanism of capitalizing the government's debt entails a cost: payment of debt service is saved now, but at the likely price of remittance of the earnings in the future of the newly privatized firms.

The additional privatizations planned for the early 1990s are likely to take place in a calmer macroeconomic environment, with greater investor confidence, a lower rate of inflation, and more order in the fiscal accounts. Such an opening is likely to lead to more benefits for both the state and society. More emphasis is now being placed on the reorganization of firms to be privatized and on design of regulatory frameworks to protect consumers while at the same time ensuring the future of the firms. But the privatization process is likely to continue at a brisk pace, as is occurring in the gas, electricity, and rail transport sectors and is about to occur in the petrochemical and iron and steel industries.

Brazil

CARLOS A. PRIMO BRAGA

After countless delays, Brazil's privatization program is finally being implemented. Announced together with President Collor de Mello's first stabilization attempt in March 1990, the program had a slow start. Its initial objective of privatizing forty-two state-owned enterprises in two years, generating US$17 billion for the quasi-bankrupt Brazilian public sector, proved too ambitious. The first major privatization of the Collor government was expected to take place in the second half of 1991. Despite the many threats still facing the Brazilian program, domestic and foreign investors are showing signs of interest in the Brazilian state-owned companies listed as candidates for privatization.

Given the poor track record of the Brazilian privatization program, the highly unstable economic environment, and the interventionist bias of the Collor administration during its first year (notwithstanding its neo-liberal rhetoric), the inevitable question is: How can the Brazilian program raise positive expectations, particularly from the point of view of foreign investors eyeing alternative privatization programs already in place in countries like Chile and Mexico?

There is no doubt that the replacement of Zelia Cardoso de Mello with Marcilio Marques Moreira as minister of the economy improved conditions for dialogue between Brazil and the international financial community. Yet the macroeconomic environment remains unstable, and there is no end in sight for the ongoing fiscal crisis. In other words, the interest in the privatization program cannot be explained by the short-run prospects of the Brazilian economy. The financial engineering of the Brazilian privatization program seems to provide the solution to this apparent puzzle.

Investors will be allowed to use several "currencies" in the auctions for the shares of the Brazilian state-owned enterprises. The possibility of using titles from the Multi-Year Deposit Facility Agreement (MYDFA), the main Brazilian title negotiated in the secondary market for sovereign debt, for instance, provides the opportunity for arbitrage. MYDFAs will be accepted in the auctions at 75 percent of their face value, while their quotation in the secondary market was around 34 cents per dollar in July 1991. In the same vein, other claims against the Brazilian government— such as privatization certificates, titles for agricultural development, and frozen *cruzados*—which are currently negotiated in secondary markets with sizable discounts, will be accepted in the auctions. Accordingly, these markets are already being affected by investors who have been preparing for the first major privatization auction, focusing on USIMINAS (Usinas Siderúrgicas de Minas Gerais, S.A.).

USIMINAS is one of the most attractive companies listed among the twenty-seven state-owned enterprises marked for privatization. A producer of flat products, with an installed capacity of 3.7 million tons of raw steel a year, USIMINAS is well known for its high standards and international competitiveness. Officially its privatization program started in June

1991 with a special offer of shares—around 10 percent of the company's total capital—to USIMINAS employees. These shares were offered at preferential prices in order to stimulate employee participation in the process despite depressed wages and the lukewarm attitude of organized labor toward the privatization program.

Foreign capital faces some restrictions in the Brazilian privatization program. Its participation cannot exceed 40 percent of the capital of the company being privatized, and profit remittances are regulated. How these restrictions will affect the participation of foreign investors is an empirical question. It is also worth mentioning that the law does not restrict future changes in ownership of a former state-owned enterprise once the privatization has been implemented. And recent developments in the secondary market for the Brazilian MYDFA suggest that foreign investors are willing to gamble on the Brazilian program.

Brazil is also being helped by the success stories of privatization in Chile and in Mexico. Foreign investors recognize that if Brazil can right its economy, then the price of the assets now being privatized may be substantially underestimated. This is not, however, a game for those with faint hearts. The privatization program itself is still threatened by disputes at the political level. In the Congress, some representatives oppose the use of MYDFAs in privatization auctions and strive for new rules of the game. Leftist parties and unions claim that the methodology adopted by the government to set the minimum selling price (based on the present value of the future flow of estimated profits) for the state-owned enterprises is a disguised way to subsidize capital. These critics argue that to build a greenfield steel plant like USIMINAS would cost some US$7 billion today; the minimum estimate, set by BNDES (Banco Nacional de Desenvolvimento Economico e Social—the national development bank in charge of the privatization program), is US$1.8 billion. This criticism assumes that the rate of return of these investments is not a relevant concept.

The uncertainty generated by the remaining political opposition has transformed the USIMINAS privatization, because of its size and the economic relevance of the company, into a major test of President Collor de Mello's program. A successful operation, however, is by no means a guarantee that the program will prosper or that it will spark a new Brazilian miracle. If the Collor administration cannot achieve macroeconomic stability while pursuing further trade liberalization, the potential benefits of the privatization program may well be lost amid the noise of existing economic distortions. In any case, risk lovers are having a great time on the eve of this new privatization round in Latin America. And it is quite clear that Brazil leaves no room for investors to adopt a cautious strategy, for the last shall be last.

Postscript

In the second half of 1991, USIMINAS and three other smaller companies were privatized. Those who opposed the privatization program achieved a Pyrrhic victory by delaying the USIMINAS auction, initially scheduled for September 24, 1991. On that day, a strident demonstration in front of Rio's stock exchange captured headlines around the world. One month later, however, USIMINAS's ordinary shares were finally negotiated, and a consortium of Brazilian banks and firms acquired control of the company by establishing an alliance with Nippon Usiminas (a minority partner controlled by Nippon Steel with an interest in the company since the 1950s) and an association of USIMINAS employees.

As a test of the soundness of Collor's privatization program, the USIMINAS case gets mixed reviews. The participation of foreign capital in the privatization, for example, was not significant—only 5 percent of the company's capital was acquired by foreign investors (the effective use of MYDFAs as a "currency" in the auction was quite limited—less than 1 percent of the total value of shares auctioned). These results suggest that foreign investors remain uncertain about the economic (and legal) prospects of Brazil's privatization program. On the positive side, it can be argued that the Collor administration demonstrated its capacity to push forward a major privatization project despite strong political opposition, opening the way for the reorganization of the Brazilian steel industry. In the first nine months of 1992, the privatization program gained speed, with eleven additional companies being privatized (including major petrochemical and steel firms). The replacement of Collor de Mello by Itamar Franco as a result of impeachment proceedings, however, has led to additional changes in the privatization procedures (such as the decision of the executive to consult with the Congress on a case-by-case basis). These changes have been interpreted by some analysts as a sign that the new administration is not particularly enthusiastic about the program. In any case, it is quite clear that the timetable and final results of Brazil's privatization program remain hostages of the country's political and macroeconomic crises.

Chile

DOMINIQUE HACHETTE AND ROLF LÜDERS

Since 1974, when Chile's massive privatization program began, some six hundred of the country's largest state-owned enterprises have been sold off, generating approximately US$2.5 billion in revenues. In addition, about half of Chile's irrigated land was allocated to laborers or poor farmers; a novel mandatory private pension scheme was institutionalized; and some elements of the education, housing, and public health systems were transferred to the private sector.

Today what was once a highly centralized mixed economy has been transformed into a modern market economy. The private sector has remained the driving force in Chile's economy after a major political transition from a military regime to an elected civilian government.

In Chile adequate regulations and controls, together with the appropriate economic policies, enabled the government to sell off a wide range of enterprises and activities. Even before privatization these regulations generated the necessary competitive environment among public companies to ensure efficiency and to set realistic prices. Since their transfer to the private sector, all divested firms have shown relatively high rates of return despite conditions that curtail their potential monopoly power. Further, funds generated by the privatization of the pension system made an enormous contribution to the development of Chile's capital market and made possible the sale of significant stock packages in some of the largest state enterprises.

Chile's state-owned enterprises were sold off in two rounds: from 1974 to 1978 and from 1985 to 1990. Methods of privatization included direct sales, bidding by auction, sales of minority packages at subsidized prices to workers, and taxpayer giveaways. During the first round of sales the Chilean government offered incentives to buyers to gain additional liquidity for the public sector in an effort to reduce the large fiscal deficit consequences of the sociopolitical crisis of 1970–1973.

This system eventually ran into problems and contributed to the deep financial crisis of 1982–1983. As a result, management of the largest privatized enterprises fell back into government hands. Those enterprises were eventually privatized again. During the next round, however, all sales were carried out on a cash basis. The lack of transparency (insufficient financial data for privatization projects) that may have deterred investors during the first round was significantly reduced by the second round and did not affect the fiscal impact of the privatization process.

On the whole, Chile's privatization program was successful in the distribution of property ownership. It stimulated the private sector to improve efficiency, it opened new investment opportunities and created new responsibilities in the private sector, and it helped reduce the country's dependency on the powerful and pervasive public sector. The process was also successful in persuading critical and strongly antagonistic groups that privatization was beneficial. By so doing, it reduced the dangers of reversibility after the transfer of power from the military government of General Augusto Pinochet to the civilian government of Patricio Aylwin.

The variety in methods of privatization ensured a balanced result for objectives as diverse as maximization of fiscal revenues and widespread property ownership. Though property distribution entailed a cost, it was tempered by the growing political support for the privatization process.

At the end of 1991, fewer than fifty enterprises remained in public hands, of which the Corporación del Cobre (CODELCO—copper), the Metro (public transportation), ENAP (petroleum), Banco del Estado (banking), and Colbún-Machicura (electricity generation) were among the most significant. Ten of the remaining state-owned enterprises were regional water and sewage utility companies. Relatively few of the big firms remaining in state hands were thus likely to be privatized. (CODELCO, valued at more than US$4 billion, requires a constitutional amendment before it can be sold.)

The privatization policy now has shifted to inviting the private sector to invest in joint ventures in existing state-owned enterprises (including public service companies) or to apply for public works concessions. The government is under growing pressure by the private sector to increase the private share in different types of infrastructure, especially in ports, which are of great importance to Chile's critical export sector. In the near future, the state will most likely divest its stock only in Empremar Sur, Ferronor Cargo, Isapre del Carbon, and Empresa Minera de Aysén and in the already privatized companies like LAN-Chile, the national airline, where it still holds a minority interest. The Congress has already approved a law, however, allowing the government to grant concessions in the case of streets, roads, ports, bridges, or public parks. The government has submitted a project to Congress to allow CODELCO to form joint ventures with national and/or foreign private partners, in which the former might even hold a majority share. The government is also seeking authority to allow the private sector to operate the cargo service of Empresa de los Ferrocarriles del Estado (the national railways). New legal instruments are not required for joint ventures with other state-owned enterprises.

The massive privatizations of the past were, as a rule, carried out by the Normalization Unit of CORFO (Corporación de Fomento de la Produccíon—the national development corporation). CORFO is likely to play a leading role in most of the future joint ventures through its Enterprises Unit managed by Eduardo Hermosilla H. The general managers of the state copper company and railways, however, will implement the joint ventures directly, while the minister of public works and the ministry staff will be responsible for concessions.

Between 1985 and 1991, 50 percent of foreign investment in shares of privatized enterprises took the form of foreign debt-equity swaps. This process reduced by one-fifth Chile's accumulated debt up to 1985 and represented 17.4 percent of the equity sold to the private sector in the divestiture of nine of the twenty-seven state firms privatized since then. The same channel was used to sell controlling interests in five firms that had been taken over by the government during the financial crisis of the early 1980s.

The high price of Chile's foreign debt paper is likely to rule out those alternatives in the future. Chile's 1974 Foreign Investment Code (DL 600) established

- repatriation of capital not earlier than three years after entry
- no mandatory fade-out requirement
- a foreign exchange regime for capital repatriation and profit remittances as favorable as that applied to the acquisition of general imports
- equal treatment for foreign investors and national investors
- no minimum time requirement and no limit on profit remittances
- no minimum time for the investment to remain in the country
- choice of tax regime on profits

A fifth of total investment in Chile during 1990 represented foreign investment. Much larger volumes have been authorized since 1985, but have not yet been carried out.

Jamaica

PETER PHILLIPS

Jamaica has made privatization one of the critical elements in its strategy to remove distortions in the economy, to increase levels of efficiency, and to foster sustained economic growth and development. The commitment to privatization is not new in Jamaica, nor is it new to the administration of Prime Minister Michael Manley. Since 1989 the government has completed an ambitious privatization program in the tourism sector. Fourteen hotels were put up for sale—with net proceeds in excess of J$882 million (US$110 million). The administration has also concluded major privatizations in the telecommunications sector. This has not only earned foreign exchange but also vastly expanded the technical and financial capabilities of this sector.

Despite these developments, however, privatization in Jamaica has been spasmodic, excessively restricted in scope, and all too often driven more by the need to balance the books than by the need for a comprehensive effort to reform the country's economic structure so that it can compete in world markets.

The scope of the current program is extensive. The government plans to divest itself of state-owned companies and of equity interests in other enterprises (there are about three hundred such cases) and to privatize certain activities that have been traditionally carried out by government. The program has two components: reorienting the public sector's role to that of an "enabler"—providing the appropriate policy framework and infrastructure to support the productive sectors—and recognizing and supporting the role of the private sector as the main vehicle for economic growth and development.

The government is compiling a comprehensive list of all the enterprises that are to be privatized. Some of these entities are in tourism, sugar, agriculture, mining and energy, utilities, and distribution and service activities. These enterprises will be privatized in phases, and no deadlines for sale or anticipation of proceeds are being set. The concept of market economics will apply in establishing the disposal prices—recognizing that investors want to earn an acceptable rate of return on their investments.

Overseas involvement is being welcomed in the privatization program, especially in cases involving foreign exchange inputs and access to advanced technology. Numerous concessions exist in the various sectors and include exemption from income and dividend taxes and reduction of or moratorium on various duties. These concessions apply for differing time periods and vary according to the industry and the activity.

Responsibility for planning, monitoring, and generally ensuring the success of the program resides in the Office of the Prime Minister. The National Investment Bank of Jamaica is the main implementing agency and is responsible for the mechanics of individual privatizations.

Mexico

ROGELIO RAMÍREZ DE LA O

In a reversal of its long tradition of heavy state intervention in economic activity, Mexico today is reprivatizing many of the more than one thousand state entities that existed in 1982. The turnaround, motivated initially by budgetary constraints, now is being pushed by an ever stronger private sector demanding that the government pull out of nonstrategic industries.

As a result of large budget deficits, caused in part by inefficient state organizations, the government in the mid-1980s signaled that it wanted to divest gradually away from manufacturing and nonstrategic areas. The policy was based on two initiatives. First, the legal framework was clarified through Article 28 of the Constitution that defined the areas of activity reserved for the state. The article excluded most manufacturing industries where state investment was substantial, although it maintained prohibitions on private participation in oil, electricity, the railways, and banking. Banking was eliminated in 1990 when the Mexican congress approved the reprivatization of commercial banks. Second, a budget program was aimed at reorganizing the finances of state organizations, reducing their debt, and increasing productivity. Although results were slow in coming, consistent budgetary control eventually achieved reduced allocations for public industrial organizations.

During the early stage of this policy the government lacked a philosophy recognizing that the private sector is the best mechanism for efficient allocation of resources. It took a long time, therefore, for the public to understand that privatizations marked a new economic policy. There were few divestitures from important enterprises in the years 1983–1988: soft drinks, hotels, and unimportant chemical, pharmaceutical, and service firms. For the same reason, labor unions did not understand that a restructuring of state organizations was absolutely essential, and conflicts between government and unions often meant that the government preferred filing for bankruptcy of the state entity rather than continuing with an operation that was losing money. Thus, many firms were first declared bankrupt and only afterward put up for sale.

The first sectors targeted were mining and manufacturing, where small firms were sold in 1988–1989. They were followed by the major sale of the Cananea copper company for over US$900 million. The Mexican government also put up for sale its ownership in the two airlines. Shipyards, trucks and engines, chemicals, sugar, and food distribution followed. Altogether these amounted to approximately US$1.6 billion.

In 1990 it became clear that the public thought well of privatizations and would support the government against strong labor unions. Part of the reason was that customers wanted better public services and considered the government a bad administrator. In 1990 the government privatized 20 percent of its stake in the telephone monopoly, TELMEX, passing its controlling share to the private sector for US$1.7 billion. This first large privatization was complex because of the need to ensure that the buyers had appropriate technology and sufficient resources for future capital expenditure. Foreigners were allowed to purchase a minority share, mainly to ensure access to technology. The success of this operation encouraged the sale in 1991 of another 26 percent of government holdings through new shares with no voting rights. Some of these shares were placed for US$1 billion in international markets. Privatizations then became an instrument for the promotion of Mexican paper in the global financial market. By 1991 only 280 enterprises remained public, down from 1,155 in 1982 (see figure 2.1 and table 2.1).

Mexico needed foreign capital, and privatization could attract it. In 1991, however, foreign participation was accepted only in nonvoting shares or in a minority capacity. This was so for the TELMEX privatization and for

Figure 2.1 Total Number of State-owned Enterprises in Mexico, 1982–1990

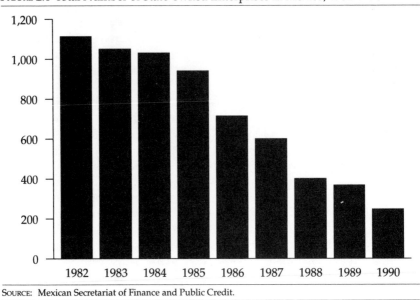

Source: Mexican Secretariat of Finance and Public Credit.

the commercial bank privatizations, where individual foreign entities could not own more than 10 percent, and total foreign ownership was limited to 30 percent. The internationalization of the economy suggests that such restrictions will become less acceptable in the future and that in coming years the preservation of niches for large Mexican conglomerates will be more difficult.

Table 2.1   Divestiture Status of State-owned Enterprises in Mexico (number of firms)

Procedure	Procedure finalized	Procedure in process	Procedure authorized
Liquidation	244	64	308
Extinction	141	14	155
Merger	82	5	87
Transfer	29	3	32
Sale	246	54	300
SOE Federal Law	69	n.a.	69
Total	811	140	951

n.a. = not available.
Source: Mexican Secretariat of Finance and Public Credit.

In addition to the US$1.6 billion received from the first, small reprivatizations through 1990, the government had by mid-1991 accumulated US$8.4 billion, of which the largest single amounts resulted from the sale of TELMEX and the Banco Nacional de México (BANAMEX). All commercial banks and other small entities were later reprivatized for US$8 billion, including the steel complex, SICARTSA, and fertilizer company (see table 2.2).

As Mexico's economy becomes more international in character, privatization objectives and policies are likely to evolve in two important ways. One is that the concept of what the state should own will be slated for revision. Another is that the role of foreign investment in privatized entities will become more significant. Nevertheless, the Mexican government has great discretionary power to outline the scope of the program in the future.

TABLE 2.2   State-owned Firms for Sale in Mexico in 1991

Industry	State-owned enterprises
Animal food	Alimentos Balanceados de México, S.A. de C.V. (plants)
Brick production	Cerámicas y Ladrillos, S.A.
Fertilizers	Fertilizantes Mexicanos (plants)
Fishing	Fisheries
Gas distribution	Distribuidora de Gas de Queretaro, S.A.
	Distribuidora de Gas del Estado de México
Gas stations	Compañía Operadora de Estaciones de Servicios, S.A. (30 gas stations)
Insurance	Aseguradora Mexicana, S.A.
Industrialized milk	Leche Industrializada Conasupo (Activos)
Mining	Minera Carbonífera Río Escondido, S.A.
Movie studios	Estudios América, S.A.
Railroad wagon construction	Constructora Nacional de Carros de Ferrocarril
Shipbuilding	Astilleros Unidos de Guaymas, S.A.
Steel	Refractarios H W Flir de México, S.A.
	Siderúrgica Lazaro Cardenas, Las Truchas
	Internacional de Aceros, S.A.
	Ferroaleaciones de México, S.A.
	Altos Hornos de México
Tourism	Nacional Hotelera de Baja California, S.A.
	Recromex, S.A. de C.V.
	Terrenos Recreo, S.A. de C.V.
	Recubrimientos y Pisos de Quintana Roo
Transportation	Servicios de Transbordadores de la Vert Caribe
	Transportes Centrales, S.A.
Zinc production	Zincamex, S.A.

SOURCE: Ministry of the Treasury, Mexico.

At the same time the internationalization of Mexico creates fresh economic forces that will be less disposed to tolerate ad hoc limitations and rules. The North American Free Trade Agreement, as part of this process, will tend to eliminate discrimination between investors. The result is likely to be a greater presence of foreign investors in activities that only a few years ago were reserved for Mexicans.

Venezuela

JOSEPH A. MANN, JR.

Venezuela's ambitious privatization program, announced with great fanfare in early 1989, is finally making progress after a slow and painful start. In August 1991 the government of President Carlos Andrés Pérez carried out its most important privatization to date, when a consortium comprising Spain's Iberia and Venezuela's Banco Provincial group won the right to purchase a majority of the shares in Venezuela's international airline, VIASA. The US$145.5 million sale will give Iberia and its partners 60 percent of VIASA's shares and significantly increase Iberia's presence in South America. Iberia, controlled by the Spanish government, already holds shares in Argentine and Chilean airlines and is discussing investments in other regional airways. After the stock purchase is completed, Iberia will hold 45 percent of VIASA's shares; the Banco Provincial Group, 15 percent; VIASA employees, 20 percent; and the Venezuelan government, 20 percent.

Before the 1991 bidding, members of the Venezuelan Congress, including members of President Pérez's own political party, Acción Democrática, faulted the government for finding only two potential bidders for VIASA: Iberia and KLM/Northwest. Critics pointed out that the government wished to privatize VIASA, but that both Iberia and KLM were government-owned or government-controlled airlines. As a result, a takeover by either of these lines would mean putting control of VIASA in the hands of a foreign government.

Until the VIASA sale the Venezuelan government had sold only three commercial banks from a list of scores of state-owned or state-controlled companies slated for privatization. These include airlines, hotels and tourist facilities, sugar mills, a shipyard, banks, water and electric power concerns, the state telecommunications company, and other public services.

In addition to selling off the three banks—Banco Occidental de Descuento, Banco Italo Venezolano, and Banco República—the government granted a concession in 1991 for private investors to operate a cellular telephone system. The administration has also been carrying out the privatization of CANTV, the state telephone and telecommunications company. The government has also asked private investors from Venezuela and overseas for tenders on Astinave, a shipyard: on management contracts for commercial ports; on a large cement company; on sugar mills; on tourist facilities (hotels and a cable car in Caracas); and on other properties.

Virtually all of the companies on the privatization hit list are money-losers. VIASA, for example, reported a net loss of US$47 million for 1990. The government is interested in finding international and domestic investors for everything it has put on the block, except for the commercial banks. Venezuelan law currently limits foreign holdings in banks to a maximum of 20 percent.

New investment and efficient management at CANTV are vital to Venezuela's economic development. The huge company (20,000 employees) provides poor service to the country's existing 1.5 million telephone subscribers and openly admits that it cannot keep up with demand for new services, especially as the economy expands. For example, international companies planning to open offices in Venezuela find that obtaining a telephone line through "normal" channels at CANTV may take up to eight years. By paying "intermediaries," however, new lines can be installed in a few days.

The Venezuelan government's minimum price for privatization of CANTV was set at US$2 billion, the highest for any company privatized in 1991. Eight international communications companies were qualified to bid for a majority share package at the telephone company. A consortium led by Bell Atlantic International bid for 40 percent of CANTV. Other bidders included American Telephone & Telegraph (AT&T), Bell Canada, France Telecom, GTE, Nippon Telephone & Telegraph, Southwestern Bell, and US West. The government required that the winning bidder make annual investments of around US$800 million and install some 300,000 new telephone lines each year.

In 1990 CANTV said that it logged an operating profit on revenues of around US$500 million. It effectively registered a US$71 million deficit, however, because of debt service and foreign exchange losses.

In June 1991 Venezuela took an important step toward privatizing its badly deteriorated telecommunications system when CANTV granted a cellular telephone concession to a private consortium for US$98 million. The winning group included Bell South (U.S.), Racal Telecom (U.K.), and three Venezuelan partners.

The privatization of CANTV was carried out successfully at the end of 1991. A consortium headed by GTE (of the United States) placed the wining bid of US$1.89 billion for 40 percent of the company's shares plus operating control. This was the largest privatization to date in Venezuela and one of the biggest anywhere. In effect, the government had set the minimum price for the company at US$2 billion, which means that the minimum price for 40 percent was US$800 million. The GTE bid exceeded the minimum by more than $1 billion. In addition to GTE, other members of the winning consortium are La Electricidad de Caracas (Venezuela's largest private utility), the Banco Mercantil group of Venezuela, Telefónica de España, and AT&T (the smallest member of the consortium).

Why has it taken so long to advance Venezuela's privatization program? The Fondo de Inversiones de Venezuela (FIV, Venezuelan Investment Fund), the government-owned financial agency charged by the Pérez administration with carrying out the privatization plan, faced a formidable task from the outset. First of all, the FIV had to draw up an accurate list of government properties (there are some four hundred ministries, government agencies, autonomous institutes, state-owned companies, and other entities in which the state is a shareholder), study the myriad legal problems associated with selling government assets, and decide on priorities and bidding procedures. Inventory was a problem because past governments in Venezuela had no clear idea of what the state actually owned.

As the FIV developed a tentative list of privatization candidates in early 1990 (major producers of red ink and public services in desperate need of reform), stiff opposition began to appear from almost every quarter. The opponents were individuals and groups who benefited in some way from the status quo at state-owned enterprises, such as company administrators, union leaders and workers, politicians who wielded influence by finding jobs for supporters and obtaining contracts for themselves and their friends, and certain business leaders who provided goods and services to these enterprises, usually using political contacts and kickbacks.

Despite the difficulties of the task and domestic opposition, however, the Venezuelan privatization program continues to move forward.

Privatization as a Remedy for State-owned Enterprises

In the 1980s the role of state-owned enterprises (SOEs) underwent close scrutiny in Latin America and in other parts of the developing world. Many governments seemed to be concluding that SOEs were not the ideal hybrids they had been made out to be: only rarely did they combine the strengths of the public and private sectors as originally expected, and occasionally they combined the worst of both. SOEs commonly failed to maximize the greater good or did so at high cost. Fine-tuning and marginal reforms had done little over the years to improve their performance, although here and there an enterprise registered remarkable results.[1]

By the late 1970s the SOE sector had absorbed a large share of the government's budget in the form of subsidies and capital infusions.[2] As governments ran into severe fiscal problems in the 1980s and encountered increasing difficulty in raising loans at home and abroad, they were forced to consider relatively radical methods for turning around the SOE sector. A program of SOE reform emerged in developing countries that had no parallel in scale and in scope in the postwar period. One class of reform—privatization—was particularly important. Its novelty is reflected in the fact that the word did not appear in standard dictionaries until the early 1980s.[3]

The pioneers of privatization were working with untested policies rather than with surefire solutions. Privatization did not consistently achieve its stated purposes. But at least the 1980s set in motion a creative search for remedies, out of which emerged a broader range of policy options than existed before. Developing countries discovered new ways to harness the private sector toward national needs and toward new public-private arrangements that could promote development.

Recent Privatization Trends

Privatization gained considerable momentum in the developing world in the 1980s. By December 1987, 571 SOEs had been privatized in 57 developing countries, according to a World Bank report (see table 3.1).[4] Transactions planned for the future, of which there were over 500 in 1988, are not included in the report. Also excluded are reprivatizations—that is, the return of recently nationalized firms to the private sector, of which there were at least several thousand cases. The World Bank labeled the cases included in table 3.1 "new privatizations." Although countries such as Chile, Bangladesh, and Israel divested some SOEs in the 1970s, privatization gained unprecedented popularity in the developing world in the 1980s.

At the same time, the evidence did not indicate that privatization was unstoppable or that the public-private balance was about to be altered dramatically in developing countries. In only a few developing countries (Chile, Côte d'Ivoire) and developed countries (the United Kingdom) had the public-private balance actually changed substantially by 1988. In many other countries often described as active privatizers, such as Mexico and Bangladesh, there were few significant cases of new privatization. To be sure, countries such as Argentina, Brazil, Malaysia, and Turkey were poised to privatize on a large scale, but the slow pace of implementation in the past raised questions about the future pace or scope of privatization in these countries.

Many of the firms privatized through 1987 were also small in size, especially in the case of private sales, which accounted for nearly half of all the cases. Privatization was also heavily concentrated in eight developing countries, which accounted for more than half the transactions in table 3.1 These countries included Brazil, Chile, and Jamaica. About half of the fifty-seven privatizing countries had fewer than five transactions completed or under way by the end of 1987.[5] Indeed, some of the countries recorded as privatizers saw their state-owned sectors expand significantly in the 1980s. Hundreds of companies fell into state ownership in Mexico as the portfolios of major banks came under state control when the banks were nationalized in 1982. And in the Philippines nonperforming assets

This chapter was adapted from Ravi Ramamurti, "The Search for Remedies," in *Privatization and Control of State-owned Enterprises*, eds. Ravi Ramamurti and Raymond Vernon (Washington, D.C.: World Bank, 1991).

TABLE 3.1 New Privatization Transactions Completed or Under Way in Developing Countries, by Region and Type, December 1987

Region	No. of countries involved	Public offering		Private sale		Sale of assets		Leasing		Management contracts		Others[a]		Total	
		Number	%	Number	%	Number	%	Number	%	Number	%	Number	%	Number	%
Sub-Saharan Africa	25	6	7.7	98	34.9	41	69.5	22	43.1	48	67.7	19	61.3	234	41.0
Asia	10	27	34.6	31	11.0	2	3.4	8	15.7	15	21.1	10	32.2	93	16.3
Pacific countries	3	1	1.3	3	1.0	0	0.0	4	7.8	2	2.8	0	0.0	10	1.8
North Africa and the Middle East	7	8	10.3	10	3.6	0	0.0	2	3.9	3	4.2	0	0.0	23	4.0
Latin America and the Caribbean	12	36	46.1	139	49.5	16	27.1	15	29.4	3	4.2	2	6.5	211	36.9
Total	57	78	100.0	281	100.0	59	100.0	51	100.0	71	100.0	31	100.0	571	100.0

NOTE: Data exclude reprivatization of recently nationalized companies and liquidations unaccompanied by sale of assets. Planned privatizations are not included in the count.
a. Includes employee buyouts, fragmentation of SOEs, and new private investment in existing SOEs.
SOURCE: Compiled from information in Charles Vuylsteke, *Techniques of Privatization of State-owned Enterprises*, vol. 1, *Methods and Implementation*, World Bank Technical Paper Number 88 (Washington, D.C., 1988), annex E, table 1, pp. 169–72.

worth $7 billion fell into government control when private firms defaulted on loans to state-owned banks.[6] In fact, the number of companies that came under state ownership in these two countries was of the same order of magnitude as the new privatizations in all other developing countries through December 1987.

Nevertheless, in both Mexico and the Philippines most of the assets that were taken over were quickly earmarked for reprivatization. At another time they might well have remained in state hands for years. More significantly, in developing countries in the 1980s few new SOEs were created as a matter of deliberate, premeditated public policy. Even though state ownership did not shrink dramatically in most countries during the 1980s, one did see an almost complete halt in the launching of new SOEs and the beginning of what had the potential to be a major reversal of ownership. Developments in the early 1990s suggest that privatization may be on the verge of explosive growth in many countries, especially within Latin America.

Forms of Privatization

In practice, privatization took many different forms, as shown in table 3.1. The term privatization has come to be used for heterogeneous policies and ideas. Some definitions of privatization are broader than that used in the World Bank survey; the term sometimes includes any policy change that enlarges the scope for private enterprise to compete with SOEs or even policies that might cause SOEs to behave more like private firms. As the definition of privatization broadens, it becomes more difficult to find a unifying theme for the variations it encompasses.

Not all forms of privatization expand the role of the private sector and shrink that of the state. Even though the term privatization sounds like the *opposite* of state ownership—attracting some followers on this basis—the actual record in developing countries reveals a more complex picture. When, for instance, a government sells a minority position in an SOE to thousands of passive investors, the state gains access to private resources without losing control over the firm. Public offerings, which accounted for 13.7 percent of all new privatizations in table 3.1, commonly fit this description, especially when large SOEs or natural monopolies are involved. Similarly, leases and management contracts, which accounted for 21.3 percent of all transactions, entail no transfer of ownership. Thus, in more than a third of all transactions—and, quite likely, in a much greater share of the assets involved—privatization altered the state's role without clearly diminishing it. The resulting organizational arrangements were hybrids, like SOEs, that combined elements of the public and private sectors. Partial privatization mixed private and state ownership; management contracts and leases mixed private management with state ownership and control; other forms mixed private ownership with state regulation.

Goals and Conflicts

Privatization was motivated by many different goals. Studies of the specific countries show that these goals included improving the government's cash flow, enhancing the efficiency of the state-owned enterprise sector, promoting "popular capitalism," curbing the power of labor unions in the public sector, redistributing incomes and rents within society, and satisfying foreign donors who wanted to see the government's role in the economy reduced. Occasionally privatization is consistent with several or all of these goals. More commonly it is not.

One common conflict is between the desire to privatize quickly and extensively and the wish to maximize proceeds from privatization. Country studies suggest that if a sufficient volume of state assets is sold, a government can rake in a tidy sum of money in the short run. The United Kingdom raised £29 billion through privatization between 1979 and 1988, while Chile raised US$850 million between 1975 and 1980.[7] Observers believe, however, that in both countries the governments realized less than they could have if privatization had been implemented more slowly and carefully.[8] Governments that were seen as strongly committed to privatization sometimes weakened their hands at the bargaining table, especially in developing countries, where the number of bidders for SOEs was usually small. In public offerings, SOE shares were often underpriced, especially if wide share ownership or a quick and "successful" sale was desired. Consider the following cases.

In Bangladesh the government returned textile enterprises to their former owners at prices equal to those at which the firms had been nationalized a decade earlier, even though the government had invested large sums in the mills in the interim.[9]

In the United Kingdom, according to one study, SOE shares were underpriced by about 51 percent on average in fixed-price public offerings, compared with 3 percent in similar private-sector offerings.[10] In addition, employees (and occasionally customers) received free or matching shares as well as subsidized credit to pay for those shares, as occurred in Jamaica.

In one case in Sri Lanka a large part of the privatization proceeds received by the government went toward severance pay for laid-off workers.[11] In other cases the government made generous concessions to the new owners, converting the loans of the SOE to equity, writing off large chunks of debt, or injecting cash into the firm before privatization. When buyers were provided credit to pay for an SOE—sometimes at subsidized rates—the government's short-run proceeds fell farther. In one case, for instance, the buyer was given fifteen years to pay 90 percent of the purchase price even though the original advertisement had called for full payment within ninety days.[12]

In Bangladesh, where twenty-two textile mills were reprivatized over just ten months, the new owners and the government haggled for years after the deals were consummated over who was responsible for what portion of the mills' debts. In the interim the private owners refused to service the disputed debt, and the threat of renationalization was hardly credible since that would have embarrassed the government and played into the hands of those who had opposed privatization in the first place.

Several other factors could also lower a government's cash realization from privatization. Sometimes workers must be assured that no one will be fired after privatization, as was the case in Bangladesh. In one instance in Malaysia the government promised that employee compensation and benefits would be maintained for at least five years after privatization for all those who chose not to accept an already generous severance package prior to the sale.[13] Bids received by the government are bound to reflect these constraints on future cost reduction. Similarly, the decisions of governments not to sell SOEs to foreigners or to certain types of local buyers (for example, ethnic Chinese in Malaysia, Asians in countries of black Africa, or associates of former president Ferdinand Marcos in the Philippines) could not fail to lower realizations from privatization.

To be sure, some of these losses may be avoided as countries gain experience with privatization, but others may be inescapable if a government wishes to move swiftly, seizing a political window of opportunity for privatization. Conversely, a government that takes all the time and care in the world to maximize proceeds from privatization may give too much time for opponents of the policy to organize their resistance. Countries like Nigeria and Turkey took several years to draw up master plans for privatization, to introduce legislation to permit divestiture, to prepare SOEs for sale, and to create organizational arrangements in government for carrying out the transactions, thus increasing the opportunities for the opposition to mobilize.[14]

To offset revenue losses from the above factors, governments may compromise on another common goal of privatization—increasing the economic efficiency of SOEs. To be sure, not all governments seem to be as concerned with efficiency as are the economists who write about privatization, but even those that are commonly mistake privatization for competition. Empirical evidence suggests that reforms designed to promote competition—or even the threat of competition—may well improve efficiency. Yet, a firm facing little or no competition will usually sell for more—and possibly sell faster—than one facing intense competition, all else being the same. When several large SOEs were privatized in the United Kingdom, various opportunities to sharpen competitive conditions were passed up, perhaps because the firms would have sold for less if those opportunities had been taken.[15]

Competition may be compromised during privatization for another reason as well: governments may prefer buyers from the same industry as the SOE because they are regarded as more likely to be able to make the firm succeed. One study of private sale transactions from six developing countries found that in 60 percent of the cases the private buyer operated in the same industry as the SOE. This figure rose to 74.2 percent in the case of developing countries.[16] In these cases competition may have been weakened rather than strengthened by privatization. Governments may have sold SOEs to such buyers because their bids were among the highest, but the highest bidder is not always the "best" bidder—that is, the one who maximizes the social value of a firm after privatization.[17]

What if competition is infeasible and undesirable, as in the case of natural monopolies? In these circumstances efficiency depends at least as much on the quality of government regulation as on the ownership of the equity. Privatization may therefore have to be accompanied by liberalization in some instances and better regulation in others to improve efficiency.[18] These conditions are not easily achieved in developing countries, however, as Mark S. Fowler and Aileen Amarandos Pisciotta point out with regard to the telecommunications industry in chapter 7. As a rule, markets are small and governments are weak. In such cases, debates on the relative merits of state versus private ownership may distract policy makers from the more important and difficult tasks of remedying market or regulatory failures.

Implementation

The implications of privatization in reality rather than in the abstract often appear to be complex and uncertain. This may be one reason why progress in carrying out privatization programs is usually so slow. Despite such problems, certain kinds of enterprises are obvious candidates for privatization in developing countries that are not driven by ideological objectives or external pressures. Examples include small SOEs operating in competitive markets, especially if they were once owned privately. Almost every developing country has at least a few such firms. Sometimes the nationalization of a large firm may have brought some small subsidiaries into state ownership. At other times a state-owned bank's decision to take over the assets of a defaulting private firm may have been the triggering event. In still other cases an industry that used to be dominated by an SOE may have evolved to include several private competitors. Sometimes SOEs can be returned to their former owners, thus shortening one of the steps involved in divestiture. Not surprisingly, many of the privatizations that occurred early in developing countries involved reprivatization or the divestiture of small SOEs. In both Brazil and Mexico, for instance, privatization in the early stages was more extensive when measured by the number of firms sold than by the magnitude or proportion of state assets divested.[19]

The largest part of the state sector in most developing countries, however, comprises state-owned enterprises that monopolize or dominate markets and that are very large by national standards. In the typical developing country, the ten or twelve largest state-owned enterprises account for 70 percent to 80 percent of the total assets of the SOE sector. In these cases privatization has been hard to evaluate and even harder to implement. As table 3.1 shows, hybrid arrangements of various kinds have been common.[20] In Latin America, where many countries had relatively well-developed capital markets, governments commonly sold a part of the equity to the public. In Africa, where capital markets were under-developed or nonexistent, governments used management contracts and leases to privatize state-owned enterprises that were large or that domi-nated their markets. The performance implications of these hybrids are far from clear. For instance, we do not know whether a mixed enterprise with minority private shareholders behaves like an enterprise wholly owned by the state, like a private enterprise, or like an enterprise distinguishable from the other categories.

Several studies have noted that privatization tends to get bogged down during its implementation.[21] Workers, managers, civil servants, and politi-cians are known to resist privatization because its costs are often concen-trated in these groups while the benefits are thinly dispersed across customers, investment bankers, and prospective buyers. Nevertheless, several case studies show that the obstacles to privatization are not insur-mountable.[22] In most countries worker support can be garnered, civil service resistance can be overcome or bypassed, managers can be induced to support the policy, buyers can be found, and capital can be raised to privatize at least a few state-owned enterprises, including some large ones. Commitment at the highest political level appears to be a necessary, though in itself insufficient, condition for seeing privatization through. Where commitment at the top is not genuine, "token privatization" may be undertaken to satisfy foreign aid donors, for instance, while studies and committee deliberations delay major moves.[23] Given commitment at the top, policy makers must choose how quickly and how openly they would like privatization to proceed. The biggest reason for privatizing quickly and secretively is that opponents are likely to be taken off guard; the downside, as we have seen, is that mistakes are likely to be made in implementation.[24]

Effects of Privatization

The indirect impact of privatization may be at least as important as the direct consequences. The privatization movement is forcing countries to reexamine the rationale for state ownership of firms, it is leading them to think more carefully before creating new state-owned enterprises, and it is inducing them to search for better management techniques. Some evidence indicates that, when a program of privatization is launched, even the performance of state-owned firms that have not been privatized improves, at least in the short run.[25] Besides, although privatization and competition are independent factors, privatization may make it easier for a government to promote competition. For example, franchising, which is one possible solution to the problem of a natural monopoly, may be infeasible if the incumbent firm is a state-owned enterprise with high exit barriers. Similarly, "yardstick competition" may be more effective if the regional monopolies belong to different owners than if they all belong to the same government.[26]

In the long run privatization is also likely to strengthen the institutions necessary to make markets work, whether through the establishment of stock exchanges, the tightening of managers' accountability to shareholders, the establishment of bankruptcy laws, or the strengthening of regulatory institutions.

Conclusion

Policy makers in Latin America and in developing countries elsewhere who wish to privatize face a difficult task. They must act in the face of incomplete understanding and information and must develop solutions that reflect the unique circumstances of individual countries or industries. Many new management practices in the private sector have evolved, however, through a similar process of trial and error, as innovative managers experimented with creative solutions to new problems, discarding those that failed and perfecting others that worked.[27]

Unfortunately, most governments stumbled into their role as owners of enterprises without much prior thought or experiment. They found themselves having to take up many commercial or quasi-commercial activities that for one reason or another were not being performed in the private sector. In pursuing those activities, governments did not wish to sacrifice the advantages they perceived as available to the autonomous firm. They therefore tried to create a hybrid institution that would combine the strengths of the public and the private sectors. With minor variations from country to country, the state-owned enterprise was considered such an institution. When the SOE concept failed to work as well as expected, however, most governments displayed limited imagination in perfecting the concept—until the fiscal pressures of the 1980s forced them to make up for lost time.

We are thus in the midst of intense experimentation with respect to SOEs. To be sure, policy makers may not think of their reform programs as experiments, but at this stage that is truly what they are. Out of those experiments may come a better understanding of how elements of the public and the private sectors can be fruitfully combined. We may learn that the ideal combination of public and private ownership varies with the size or strategic significance of a firm, the structure of its market, the depth and capabilities of the private sector, and the quality of government regulation. If the United Kingdom served as the laboratory of privatization for the industrial world. Latin America is doing the same for the developing world, especially with regard to natural monopoly industries (power, telecommunications, transportation).[28] International sharing of the lessons of such experiments will help to speed the learning process.

Notes

1. Widespread disappointment over the performance of SOEs is seen in public reports in various developing countries, including Brazil, Bangladesh, India, South Korea, and several countries of sub-Saharan Africa. On the latter, see John Nellis, "Public Enterprise in Sub-Saharan Africa," World Bank Discussion Paper 1 (Washington, D.C., 1986).

2. SOEs were estimated to contribute substantially to public sector deficits and to have typically financed less than one-fifth of their investments through internally generated resources. See Govindan Nair and Anastasios Filippides, "How Much Do State-owned Enterprises Contribute to Public Sector Deficits in Developing Countries—and Why?" World Bank Policy, Planning, and Research Working Paper, WPS 45 (Washington, D.C., December 1988). For an empirical confirmation of the key role of financial factors in promoting privatization in developing countries, see Ravi Ramamurti, "Why Are Developing Countries Privatizing?" *Journal of International Business Studies* 23, no. 2 (1992), pp. 225–50.

3. *Webster's New Collegiate Dictionary* included the word privatization for the first time in its 1983 edition, according to *Prospects for Privatization*, ed. Steve H. Hanke (New York: American Political Science Academy Press, 1988), p. 2.

4. Charles Vuylsteke, *Techniques of Privatization of State-owned Enterprises*, vol. 1, *Methods and Implementation*, World Bank Technical Paper Number 88 (Washington, D.C., 1988), table 1, pp. 169–72.

5. Vuylsteke, *Techniques of Privatization*.

6. Stephan Haggard, "The Philippines: Picking Up after Marcos," in *The Promise of Privatization: A Challenge for American Foreign Policy*, ed. Raymond Vernon (New York: Council on Foreign Relations, 1988), p. 98.

7. On the United Kingdom, see Yair Aharoni, "The United Kingdom: Transforming Attitudes," in Raymond Vernon, *The Promise of Privatization*, pp. 25–26. On Chile, see Helen Nankani, *Techniques of Privatization of State-owned Enterprises*, vol. 2, *Selected Country Case Studies*, World Bank Technical Paper Number 89 (Washington, D.C., 1988), p. 19.

8. On the United Kingdom, see John Vickers and George Yarrow, *Privatization: An Economic Analysis* (Cambridge, Mass.: MIT Press, 1988). On Chile, see Pan A. Yotopoulos, "The (Rip)Tide of Privatization: Lessons from Chile," *World Development* 17, no. 5 (1989), pp. 683–702.

9. Klaus Lorch, "Privatization through Private Sale: The Bangladeshi Textile Industry," in *Privatization and Control of State-owned Enterprises*, eds. Ravi Ramamurti and Raymond Vernon (Washington, D.C.: World Bank, 1991), pp. 116–42.

10. See Rama Seth, "Distributional Issues in Privatization," *Federal Reserve Bank of New York Quarterly Review* (Summer 1989), p. 34. The 51 percent figure excludes the privatization of British Petroleum. The 3 percent figure for private sector initial offerings is the average for the period 1983–1985.

11. The company involved was Noorani Tiles, as reported in Nankani, *Techniques of Privatization*, p. 118.

12. Nankani, *Techniques of Privatization*.

13. Roger Leeds, "Malaysia: Genesis of a Privatization Transaction," *World Development* 17, no. 5 (1989), pp. 741–56.

14. See Roger Leeds, "Turkey: Rhetoric and Reality," in Vernon, *The Promise of Privatization*, pp. 149–78, especially pp. 159–69.

15. See Vickers and Yarrow, *Privatization: An Economic Analysis*, pp. 426–29.

16. Seth, "Distributional Issues in Privatization," table 12, p. 37.

17. For a detailed discussion of this point, see Leroy James, Pankaj Tandon, and Ingo Vogelsang, "Selling State-owned Enterprises: A Cost-Benefit Approach," in *Privatization and Control of State-owned Enterprises*, eds. Ramamurti and Vernon, pp. 20–44.

18. See, for instance, Vickers and Yarrow, *Privatization: An Economic Analysis*. The authors assert that "the degree of product market competition and the effectiveness of regulatory policy typically have rather larger effects on performance than ownership *per se*" (p. 3).

19. On privatization in Brazil, see Ethan B. Kapstein, "Brazil: Continued State Dominance," in Vernon, *The Promise of Privatization*, pp. 122–48. The election of a conservative president in 1989 showed promise of raising the ambitiousness of Brazil's privatization program.

20. Although the World Bank survey did not distinguish between public offerings in which the government sold all its equity and those in which only a portion was sold, a review of individual cases in the report's appendix indicates that

partial divestiture was by far the most common case, especially when large SOEs were concerned.

21. See, for instance, James E. Austin, Lawrence H. Wortzel, and John F. Coburn, "Privatizing State-owned Enterprises: Hopes and Realities," *Columbia Journal of World Business* 21, no. 3 (Fall 1986), pp. 51–60.

22. Several country studies, including those contained in Ramamurti and Vernon, *Privatization and Control of State-owned Enterprises*, describe how the obstacles to privatization were surmounted.

23. This may have been the case in some African countries, according to Thomas M. Callaghy and Ernest James Wilson III, "Africa: Policy, Reality, or Ritual?" in Vernon, *The Promise of Privatization*, pp. 179–230.

24. Côte d'Ivoire appears to have taken an ad hoc approach guided by the case-by-case decisions of the country's president. See Callaghy and Wilson, "Africa: Policy, Reality, or Ritual?" pp. 202–7.

25. See George Yarrow, "Privatization in Theory and Practice," *Economic Policy* 2 (1986), pp. 324–77.

26. "Franchising" refers to the strategy of auctioning the right to provide a (natural) monopoly service. Franchising creates competition *for* the market when competition *in* the market is infeasible or undesirable. "Yardstick competition" is a method for promoting competition among several regulated, regional monopolies, such as regional electricity companies. For a succinct review of these concepts, see Vickers and Yarrow, *Privatization: An Economic Analysis*, pp. 110–19.

27. For an excellent study of organizational learning in the private sector, see Alfred D. Chandler, *Strategy and Structure: Chapters in the History of the American Industrial Enterprise* (Cambridge, Mass.: MIT Press, 1962).

28. For recent studies of privatization in Latin America and its expeditionary character, see the special issue on privatization of *Latin Finance* (March 1991) and Ravi Ramamurti, "Privatization and the Latin American Debt Problem," in *Private Sector Solutions to the Latin American Debt Problem*, ed. Robert Grosse (Miami: North-South Center, University of Miami, 1992), pp. 153–76.

Privatization Requirements of Foreign Investors

The revolutions that swept Eastern Europe in the winter of 1989 caused international attention to be focused on the dynamics of the shift from centrally planned to free-market economies. Many observers, politicians, and citizens believe that the privatization of state-owned enterprises (SOEs) is essential to this shift, as it will eliminate inefficiency and waste in the economy and will create a robust Western-style private sector complete with stock exchanges, private banks, open currency exchanges, and the relatively free trade of goods and services. Privatization cannot be seen as a panacea for underdevelopment, however. Nations in Latin America and elsewhere have found that in order to succeed, a privatization program must be an integral part of a much more comprehensive package of reforms aimed at rebuilding and improving the economic, political, and legal infrastructure.

Governments find it tempting to treat privatization separately because it can generate a significant inflow of funds to the government. In Eastern Europe, for example, national governments are estimated to have more than US$100 billion in assets to sell to investors. Cash-hungry governments worldwide are eager to sell their assets as soon as possible and redirect the money toward accelerating their countries' economic and social development. A critical decision is how to minimize the financial

The author gratefully acknowledges the assistance of Anne Nisenson in the preparation of this chapter.

and social costs of dislocation caused by economic restructuring, of which privatization is only a part.

The reality in many Latin American nations and in Eastern Europe, however, is that the local population does not hold anywhere near US$100 billion in savings and does not have access to mechanisms through which it could raise even a fraction of that amount. To circumvent this structural obstacle, governments have devised a number of methods to increase large- and small-scale domestic investment in privatized state-owned enterprises. In Chile, for example, small domestic investors were allowed to purchase shares with just a 5 percent down payment, with the balance to be paid over fifteen years at a 0 percent real interest rate. In addition, small investors were given a 30 percent discount for timely payment of debt and were permitted to use up to 20 percent of the investment as a tax credit against future income taxes.[1] (See chapter 6, "Financial Incentives for Investment in Chile's Privatization," for a more extensive discussion of these incentives.) Other nations, those in Eastern Europe in particular, have experimented with the wide distribution of vouchers redeemable for shares in privatized companies in order to spur local involvement and to avoid concentration of ownership.

Even when sufficient capital can be generated in the domestic market, however, the fact remains that debt-led privatization programs, especially in countries with modest domestic financial sectors, are problematic and involve a costly and long-term sustained commitment on the part of investors. There is also the risk that the enterprise will again become an obligation of the government.

Small domestic investors and local capital markets are often stretched to their financial limits just to participate in the initial privatization of an enterprise. In a nation with limited access to credit, an enterprise thus privatized will be especially vulnerable in times of recession or if increased industry competitiveness requires investment in modernization or expansion. Individual domestic investors in developing nations simply do not have pockets as deep or access to credit as convenient as large foreign multinationals or institutional investors.

Foreign investment can be an important contributor to a successful privatization effort. In Chile, for instance, which has focused intensively on motivating domestic investment, enterprises financed with foreign capital were clearly more resistant to failure or renationalization.[2] According to a World Bank study, several factors account for the failure of debt-led privatization in Chile:

- a failure to screen potential buyers and the consequent sale of enterprises to investors lacking adequate financial bases and technical and managerial expertise

- an excessively large scale of divestiture compared with the limited capacity of the domestic financial market

- a heavy reliance on debt as an instrument for financing the sale of shares

- the 1982–1983 recession, which may have been worsened by the first and second privatizations, which took place in 1974–1975 and 1975–1979[3]

Although foreign investment does not necessarily constitute the majority of investment in the privatization programs of developing nations, it is an important capital reservoir. It is accompanied by a steady inflow of technology and business acumen that is often severely lacking, especially in privatizing the largest state-owned enterprises. Manuel Suárez-Mier, the minister for economic affairs at the Mexican Embassy in Washington, D.C., underlined the importance of foreign investment "in the generation of resources required to carry out the whole plan, but also . . . in [its] crucial contribution towards the modernization of the country's productive plant through the transfer of innovative technology and organizational skills."[4] The World Bank also finds that "the problem in many economies will be that there are only a small number of corporate investors with the financial resources and management experience required to acquire larger SOEs."[5]

Much has been written about what elements privatization programs must encompass if they are to be palatable to local populations. The essential question of the needs and requirements of foreign investors, however, has been ignored in much of the literature and in the development of specific privatization programs. In Brazil, for example, a World Bank study found that "[f]oreign investors were not explicitly included in the privatization program because the role of foreign capital in the Brazilian economy, as elsewhere, has long been an emotional and hotly debated topic."[6]

Some concerns implicit in the reluctance of governments to make foreign investment the centerpiece of their privatization programs are that foreign investors may obtain a monopolistic or oligopolistic position; they may reduce industrial possibilities for domestic companies; and they may aggressively repatriate capital rather than promote national economic and social goals. These concerns apply to foreign investment in general, not just to investments associated with privatization programs.

Like other investors, foreign investors in privatization programs seek to maximize return while minimizing risk to their investment. They will carefully analyze the macroeconomic and regulatory environment of a nation when making decisions about where and when to allot funds. Required preconditions are common to foreign investors in general and are separate from the specific conditions of the state-owned enterprise to be privatized. This chapter outlines some important elements in a privatization program that will more likely attract significant levels of foreign investment.

Macroeconomic Considerations

Investors look for *strong and stable economic indicators*—the prospect of sustained economic growth, moderate inflation, positive interest rates, stable wages, and a stable exchange rate policy.

Reliable and consistent pricing and valuation of the enterprise will be possible only with the existence of *relatively developed capital markets*. Capital markets will also provide a mechanism for institutional investors, who are not interested in the actual day-to-day operations of an enterprise, to enter the market and to place their capital at the disposal of newly privatized entities.

In the absence of advanced capital markets, which will admittedly take many years to develop, national governments could pursue policies that would create a competitive, two-tiered banking system in which commercial banks are capable of assessing risk and providing investment capital.

To ensure that foreign investors will not continually be the only source of funding for future improvements or expansion, there must be some confidence that *needed capital* can be found within the domestic economy. Brazil is an example of the absence of this liquidity. Although the country has sufficient domestic financial assets to fund a large part of its privatization program, "additional new investment, considered by many essential for future growth of the Brazilian economy, will have to be financed by additional savings, internal or external."[7]

Other characteristics investors will look for include fiscal and monetary *policies that favor price stability* and government relationships with multilateral donor agencies and international banks that provide some measure of *international creditworthiness*. *Demographic characteristics*—such as the size of the workforce, age distribution, and education levels—*must complement business needs*. Governments must encourage *relatively open market regimes* for the pricing of final goods and factors of production and an *explicit automatic pricing system* for natural monopolies (such as electric utilities).

Political Considerations

Foreign investors will be guided in their decisions by the existence of certain political conditions. Foremost among these is the *stability of the government*. The investor must have confidence that the government can formulate realistic goals and follow through on its promises. Perhaps most important to foreign investors is belief in the government's commitment to privatization as part of a permanent restructuring of the economy. Perception of risk is greatly increased if privatization is pursued only to raise revenue because this makes it more likely that an industry could be renationalized in the future. This is a significant problem in Latin America. Suárez-Mier has stated that Mexico's privatization programs have been pursued as part of the "macroeconomic and structural reform effort undertaken by the Mexican authorities to confront the economic crisis which resulted from the abrupt termination of the country's international credit flows."[8] Such a statement would give much more confidence to the foreign investor than the Brazilian objective to "raise revenue in order to retire part of the budget deficit and to avert needed investment expenditures in SOEs, in order to avoid further deficit financing."[9]

Companies will look for *freedom from excessive political risk*. They want to be free from the fear of expropriation or other measures affecting the ability of investors to control and operate their assets. The perception of this risk can be minimized by using investment guaranteeing organizations such as the Overseas Private Investment Corporation (OPIC), the Multilateral Investment Guarantee Agency (MIGA), or the International Finance Corporation's Guaranteed Recovery of Investment Principal (GRIP). Each of these entities guarantees foreign investment against noncommercial risk.

Investors will also need *flexible regulations but clear guidelines* backed by explicit laws governing foreign investments and privatization and a *clear and open policy-making process*. Transparency in restructuring, pricing, and selling SOEs is important to maintain confidence and competition in individual transactions. A public policy process that is structured and follows clear guidelines and regulations and that is not arbitrary, secretive, or personalized achieves the same goal.

Government support for private business, including a functioning and cooperative bureaucracy, will be an important consideration for investors. Other characteristics will include a *tax system that does not penalize foreign investment* and a *foreign policy that does not create conflicts with private businesses* that have diversified markets and sources of supply. For example, will the government's foreign policy preclude certain supply or market arrangements with subsidiaries or other business abroad?

The country should encourage *a favorable legal environment for business*. This would include creating the equivalent of the U.S. Commercial Code, so that the growing private sector has some legal framework and is not a "Wild West," where anything goes.

Regulations and mechanisms must allow for the repatriation of capital dividends and other funds, placing *few restrictions on the percentage of shares of a company that can be purchased.* Most state-owned enterprises need major overhaul to be profitable in competitive markets. Investors will want to be closely involved with the management of the company and will expect to be able to purchase a controlling interest. The much-publicized sale of 70 percent of Skoda, the Czechoslovak automotive company, to Volkswagen is a clear example of this trend. Central to Volkswagen's investment plan was a major restructuring of Skoda, including the introduction of several completely new lines of automobiles. If the country has a stock market that is large enough to float the shares of the company, or if this can be accomplished on a foreign stock exchange, it will be more attractive and more accessible to institutional and fund investors, and issues of majority ownership may not be as compelling.

Investors will expect the country to use *generally accepted accounting standards* to ensure that the stated value of a company is comparable to others within the country and abroad and to allow predictions to be made regarding potential returns on investment. They will also expect to have *access to reliable, consistent, and comparable financial information* and *guarantees that the buyer has clear title to purchased property.*

Finally, investors will look for *immigration regulations that do not curtail foreign management participation.* In almost all nations that contemplate privatization programs as vehicles for economic development, one of the most critical limiting factors is the shortage of skilled employees capable of understanding and implementing the technical and financial changes that will be necessary first to privatize enterprises and then to make them viable in the long run. Often various employees, ranging from line managers to financial analysts to accountants and auditors, must be imported. This is particularly important when the intent of a foreign investor is to restructure the entity. Relatively free access to technically qualified foreign personnel for more than just training programs is essential to build confidence that the investor will have some control over the investment.

These factors can provide a standardized framework that allows foreign investors interested in newly privatized enterprises to assess their risks. Expecting 100 percent satisfaction with these conditions is clearly wishful thinking, but foreign investors will weigh alternative investment opportunities with these factors in mind. Privatization programs have expanded tremendously in the late 1980s and early 1990s, and sellers now outnumber buyers. The more a country meets these conditions, the more likely it is that foreign investors will participate in the country's privatization efforts.

Examples from the Field

The elements that compose this framework are not new; many investment decisions by foreign companies have been made based on similar calculations of risk. Large multinational firms that have already made significant investments in foreign privatization programs have geared the degree of their investment to a conscious assessment of the overall macroeconomic and political climate in the potential host nation.

One striking example of the effect that national environment can have on investment decisions is the case of Bell Atlantic International's investments in the privatization programs of three very different nations.

- *New Zealand.* Because the country has a stable currency, imposes no limit on foreign ownership or repatriation of capital, and has international political clout and a stable domestic political situation, Bell Atlantic chose to purchase 100 percent of a state-owned enterprise that was being offered to the private sector.

- *Czechoslovakia.* A more unstable and inconvertible currency, the national government's weak commitment to its own privatization program, and questions about the viability of equipment and the labor force diminished investor confidence. Bell Atlantic decided to make only a small percentage investment.

- *Argentina.* The wild currency fluctuations, feeble economic policy, and mercurial political situation in Argentina almost drove Bell Atlantic away altogether. The company has said that it would only manage another company's investment, not make any investment itself, because of the volatility of the national climate.

Governments that ignore the requirements of foreign investors risk losing investor confidence and thereby a major source of revenue. One such example, which underlines the importance of a well-considered privatization strategy, is the case of a Swiss investment in a state-owned hotel in Hungary that was privatized. To execute the privatization, the Swiss made a major investment, at a given price per share, in the hotel. The day following the share purchase, the share price more than doubled on the local exchange. Even though this value increase was probably due in large part to the Swiss involvement, it was seen as unjust. As a result, a suit was brought challenging the privatization, and the transaction was voided. The negative impact on foreign investment is clear: as they say, once burned, twice shy.

One can cite other examples: Argentina's recent success in using debt-equity swaps to attract foreign investment to privatization transactions as in the ENTEL case, in which the country canceled US$5.03 billion of its outstanding debt to the commercial banks (7.7 percent of its US$65 billion external debt; see figures 4.1 and 4.2). The Argentine example contrasts with the unwillingness of countries such as Brazil (even though a new program has been set up) to take advantage of debt-equity swaps to achieve their privatization objectives. Hungary has allowed unlimited repatriation of capital and profit from privatization investments by foreigners and guaranteed access to foreign exchange. The more common practice is to limit one or the other with lesser involvement by foreign investors in a country's privatization efforts.

FIGURE 4.1 The Restructuring and Privatization of ENTEL, November 1990

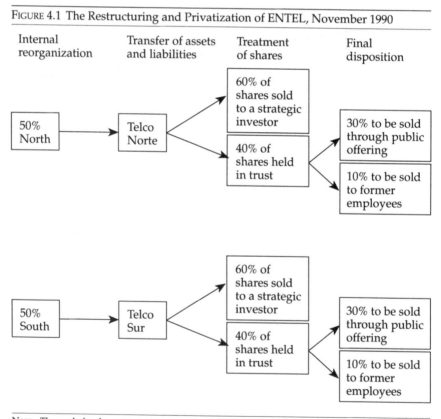

NOTE: The goals for the restructuring were to reduce the size of the entity to be sold, to recapitalize to reduce values of equity, and to sell only controlling interest to reduce the investment required.
SOURCE: Price Waterhouse International Privatization Group.

FIGURE 4.2 Structuring of the ENTEL Deal, 1990

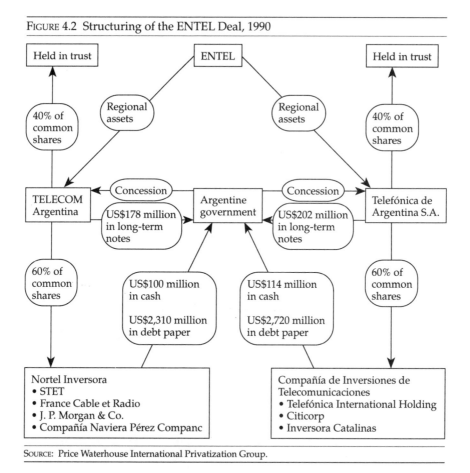

SOURCE: Price Waterhouse International Privatization Group.

Privatization can be a win-win proposition given the correct variables, among which the choice of strategy is crucial. Privatization strategies that minimize investor risk can compensate for macroeconomic and political weaknesses within a nation. The success of Chile compared with the records of Brazil and Argentina attests to the validity of this point.

Conclusion

Investors in privatization programs are essentially operating in the absence of complete information. As a result, any outcome is seen as an important precedent on which to make future cost-benefit calculations, and programs are under intense pressure to achieve immediate success. But this need, coupled with the tendency of privatization authorities to promise too much too soon, creates a recipe for disaster. Privatization programs should take a lesson from Chile that "privatization on an extensive scale is best avoided, especially where the financial and capital markets are weak."[10]

Participation by foreign investors in privatization programs is essential both to ensure an adequate amount of capital to make privatization possible and to infuse obsolete industries with modern management and production techniques. This in turn will improve enterprise efficiency and increase profitability. Privatization can be a positive-sum game for government, investors, workers, and the population at large. Since foreign investment will play a crucial role in achieving many of their objectives, privatization programs should specifically encourage foreign participation.

Notes

1. Helen Nankani, *Techniques of Privatization of State-owned Enterprises*, vol. 2, *Selected Country Case Studies*, World Bank Technical Paper Number 89 (Washington, D.C., 1988), p. 30.

2. Nankani, *Techniques of Privatization*, pp. 42–45.

3. Nankani, *Techniques of Privatization*, pp. 27–28.

4. Manuel Suaréz-Mier, *The Mexican Privatization Program: Ten Questions and One Case Study*, paper given at the International Privatization Investment Opportunities Conference, New York, February 20–21, 1991, p. 10.

5. Charles Vuylsteke, *Techniques of Privatization*, vol. 1, *Methods and Implementation*, World Bank Technical Paper Number 88 (Washington, D.C., 1988), p. 126.

6. *Brazil, Prospects for Privatization*, World Bank Internal Paper (Washington, D.C., June 30, 1989), p. 45.

7. *Brazil, Prospects for Privatization*, p. 51.

8. Suaréz-Mier, *The Mexican Privatization Program*, p. 1.

9. *Brazil, Prospects for Privatization*, p. 11.

10. Nankani, *Techniques of Privatization*, p. 40.

Foreign Direct Investment in Latin America's Privatization

Privatization is not a new phenomenon in Latin America. An early case of public equity sales can be found as early as the 1960s in the Dominican Republic.[1] In more recent times two waves of privatization emerged in the region: the first, in the mid-1970s, took place almost exclusively in Chile; and the second, beginning in the mid-1980s, continues to the present.[2] The second has been far more extensive than previous privatizations in regard to the number of countries involved, the number of state-owned enterprises for sale, the size of those companies, and the amount of each sale.

Since the mid-1980s the offering of state assets to private investors has been spiraling. By 1990 nearly US$5 billion of state equities had been sold to the private sector. The leading countries in this second wave have been Mexico and Argentina, with sales of US$2.47 billion and US$2.29 billion, respectively. The sale of state equities has contributed considerably to the overall increase of private foreign investment in the region, which rose from US$15 billion in 1989 to US$24 billion in 1990. Further, the progressive consolidation of economic stability in several countries and the attractive profits offered by local stock markets have created a massive inflow of foreign capital into Latin America.[3]

This chapter considers the amount of private investment that the sale of state-owned enterprises has attracted and the accompanying role of foreign direct investment (FDI), building on the links between privatization programs in Latin America and new flows of foreign direct investment to the region. It also presents the participation of foreign direct investment for many of the most recent and relevant privatized companies.[4] Because the telecommunications sector has played the most important role in privatization programs throughout the region, the sale of state-owned telephone companies and other related industries is emphasized. Also discussed are privatization of other key economic sectors, such as aviation, railways, oil and petrochemicals, banking, steelworks, and tourism. Some countries, such as Argentina, Mexico, and Chile, will be explored more thoroughly than others because privatization there is more advanced and the reforms more significant. The later privatizers, such as Brazil, Bolivia, Ecuador, Uruguay, and Venezuela are also described.

The last section is devoted to the analysis of current academic and political controversies on foreign capital inflows to less-developed economies. Advocates and critics of foreign direct investment present both the traditional terms of the debate and some new elements related to current issues such as debt-equity swap privatizations.

Mexico

Mexico, like many other Latin American countries, showed impressive growth in the period after World War II. The economy grew at a rate of 6.6 percent from 1960 to 1976 and 8.4 percent from 1977 to 1981. Like many other countries in the region, however, a sharp economic crisis in 1982 ushered in a period of stagnation and recession. In the subsequent years the burden of a mounting external debt, drops in international prices for petroleum, rising rates of inflation, and the convergence of various other negative factors signaled to Mexican leaders that it was time for a change. The failure of early minor reforms showed that the magnitude of the crisis necessitated major structural reforms.

In its effort to overcome the crisis, the government implemented a profound restructuring of the economy based on three main transformations: state reform (privatization of state-owned enterprises), opening of the economy (liberalization and trade reforms), and incentives for private sector growth (new, more lenient regulations for foreign and local investments).

Beginning in 1983 and continuing through the present, the privatization program reduced the number of state-controlled institutions from 1,228 to 264. By mid-1991, 826 state-owned enterprises had been transferred to the private sector, and 138 more were slated to be privatized, liquidated, merged, or dissolved in the near future (see figure 5.1).

Liberalizing the economy was the second major task. The program started in 1983. In the first two years of implementation the percentage of import value subject to licensing was reduced from 83 percent to 37

FIGURE 5.1 Divestiture of State-owned Enterprises in Mexico,
December 1982–March 1991

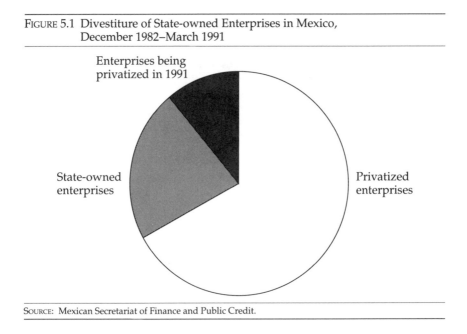

Enterprises being
privatized in 1991

State-owned
enterprises

Privatized
enterprises

SOURCE: Mexican Secretariat of Finance and Public Credit.

percent. By 1987 import tariffs ranged from 0 to 20 percent. By 1990 the
Mexican economy qualified as one of the most open economies in the
world: the average tariff was 13.1 percent, import licensing was required for
only 2 percent of the tariff items, and the economic sectors that still
required import licensing (automobiles and pharmaceuticals) were gradually being liberalized.

The third goal was the expansion of the private sector. When President
Carlos Salinas de Gortari took office in December 1988, his economic team
realized that the country would need to attract massive amounts of foreign
direct investment—US$30 billion in the following six years—to achieve the
government's macroeconomic objectives. Accordingly, the Salinas administration put into effect, on May 16, 1989, a drastic revision of the Mexican
investment regulations. The existing 1973 "Law to Promote Mexican Investment and Regulate Foreign Investment" was modified to "increase the
volume and accelerate the flow of investment capital by providing legal
certainty and by simplifying and clarifying the administrative rules and
procedures that apply to such transactions."[5]

These new regulations are an effort to liberalize the investment environment. Foreign investors may own up to 100 percent of those businesses
classified as unrestricted. Projects in most economic sectors are no longer
subject to approval by the National Foreign Investment Commission

(CNIE). Authorization is automatic as soon as the project meets certain basic requirements: investment should not exceed US$100 million; funds should come from abroad; the project must not be located in one of Mexico's largest metropolitan areas; there should not be significant foreign exchange inflows or outflows over the project's first three years; and the project must use adequate technology, satisfy environmental requirements, create jobs, and offer employee training and personnel development programs.

New foreign investment regulations also categorize economic activities as to whether foreign participation is limited or not. Activities listed as "classified" are categorized as follows:[6]

System 1: Activities reserved for the state

- extraction of petroleum, basic petrochemical activities, and natural gas and petroleum refining

- extraction and/or use of uranium and radioactive minerals

- uranium treatment and uses of nuclear fuels

- generation, transmission, and supply of electrical energy

- railway transportation

- telegraphs

- minting coins

- banking, funds, and financial trusts

System II: Activities reserved for Mexicans

- forestry and forest nurseries

- retail sales of liquid gas

- auto-freight transportation services

- coastal maritime transportation

- transportation service on Mexican registry airplanes and air taxis

- credit institutions other than banks, funds, and financial trusts

- services of stock brokerages, stock exchange investment companies, bond and insurance institutions, and independent pension funds

- transmission of radio and television programs

- notaries, customs agencies, and similar representatives

- administration of maritime, lake, and river ports

System III: Foreign investment allowed up to 34 percent

- exploitation and/or use of carbon and minerals containing iron
- extraction and/or use of phosphoric rock and sulfur

System IV: Foreign investment allowed up to 40 percent

- secondary petrochemicals
- manufacture and assembly of automotive parts and accessories

System V: Foreign investment allowed up to 49 percent[7]

- extraction and/or use of metallic minerals not containing iron other than uranium and radioactive minerals
- extraction and/or use of nonmetallic minerals
- extraction and/or use of rocks, clays, and sands
- manufacture of explosives and fireworks
- manufacture of firearms and cartridges
- fishing and aquaculture
- internal port and river and lake transportation services
- telecommunications services, excluding telegraphs
- rental agencies

System VI: Foreign investment allowed up to 100 percent[8]

- agriculture, such as the felling of trees and collection of forest products
- livestock and game
- newspaper and magazine publication
- carbon derivates (coke and others)
- building, construction, and installation
- maritime transportation services on the high seas
- administration of roads, bridges, and auxiliary services
- air navigation services and administration of airports and heliports
- vehicle-towing services

- operating and investment company services
- private education
- legal, accounting, and auditing services
- services related to financial, insurance, and bond institutions

These new regulations have created a new opening for the participation of foreign capital in Mexico. Some economic analysts believe, however, that the reforms have not been radical enough. Incoming foreign capital flows have been meager and decreasing in recent years. While in 1987 Mexico attracted US$3.2 billion in foreign direct investment, foreign direct investment dropped to US$2.5 billion in 1989 and reached only US$983 million during the first half of 1990. From this perspective, the fact that foreign capital is accepted in some important sectors only with a minority share or in nonvoting shares has presumably kept foreign direct investment away from Mexican borders. Some attribute foreign reluctance to invest in Mexico to the fact that the 1973 Investment Law, which is not very lenient with foreign capital, is still the main valid legal instrument for investment in Mexico despite benefits granted by the 1989 regulations. Some Asian investors have indicated that Mexico has not yet proved that current economic trends will translate into long-term stability. All these factors affect the confidence of capitalists from abroad in the Mexican market.

This skittishness on the part of foreign investors seemed to have vanished in the last half of 1990. By the end of the year, foreign direct investment had skyrocketed to US$4.2 billion, and it reached US$8.0 billion in the first half of 1991.[9] In the near future we should expect, if not a more extensive participation of foreign capital in the Mexican economy, at least a certain stability in the incoming flows of foreign direct investment. Two factors seemed to be working toward the consolidation of this emerging trend. First, as Mexico's economy becomes more liberalized and open, pressures to allow extensive participation of foreign capital in Mexican businesses will increase, stimulating legal changes in favor of foreign direct investment. Second, the expected implementation of the North American Free Trade Agreement (NAFTA) will tend to unify legal treatment of local and foreign businesses and will probably add more stability to the Mexican economy.[10]

A broad look at the evolving patterns of foreign direct investment in recent years shows that privatization has helped to reverse a low degree of foreign participation in the Mexican economy. The sale of state-owned enterprises has attracted a considerable amount of investment from abroad and created a favorable environment for business.

Telecommunications

Telecommunications has been a key element in Salinas's modernization strategy since his electoral campaign. As early as 1987 he claimed that "telecommunications will become the cornerstone of the program to modernize Mexico's economy."[11] Faithful to his assertion, Mexico embarked two years later on the sale of the second largest company in the country and one of the thirty largest companies in the world, Teléfonos de México, S.A. (TELMEX).

The privatization of TELMEX was divided into two clearly defined stages. The first involved the sale of the controlling share of the company to a private consortium of Mexican and foreign companies; the second concerned the financial operations required to offer TELMEX shares in the international stock market.

The privatization of TELMEX, along with that of ENTEL (Argentina), emerged in 1990 as one of the most interesting deals concerning foreign direct investment in Latin America. As Eugene Laborne, vice president of Nynex International asserted: "the privatization of TELMEX is a unique opportunity in life, it could become the deal of the century."[12] The bidding process for Mexico's telephone company initially attracted sixteen of the most qualified international telecommunications companies, including Nippon Telephone and Telegraph, Cable and Wireless Plc., Southwestern Bell Co., Nynex International, GTE Telephone Co., Bell Canada, Singapore Telecom, US Sprint, Telefónica de España, France Cable et Radio, STET, and United Telecommunications.

On December 13, 1990, one month after the November 15 bidding deadline, TELMEX was sold to a consortium comprising the financial Carso Group (Mexico) and two foreign common carriers, Southwestern Bell (U.S.) and France Cable et Radio (a subsidiary of France Telecom). The government sold privileged type AA shares representing 20.4 percent of the company's capital but equal to 51 percent of the company's voting shares to the consortium for US$1.76 billion. Because of restrictions imposed by the Foreign Investment Law, Carso Group has control of the company with 10.4 percent of the shares; Southwestern Bell and France Cable et Radio own 5 percent each.[13]

The amount of foreign direct investment received by the Mexican government for TELMEX exceeded expectations. The TELMEX sale was, however, enhanced by bundling in the same deal a variety of related companies, such as Anuncios en Directorios, S.A.; Compañía de Teléfonos y Bienes Raíces, S.A. de C.V.; Construcciones Telefónicas Mexicanas, S.A. de C.V.; Canalizaciones Mexicanas, S.A. de C.V.; Construcciones y Canalizaciones, S.A. de C.V.; Alquiladora de Casas, S. A. de C.V.; Editorial Argos, S.A.; Fuerza y Clima, S.A.; Imprenta Nuevo Mundo, S.A.;

Impulsora Mexicana de Telecomunicaciones, S.A.; Industrial Afiliada, S.A. de C.V.; Operadora Mercantil, S.A.; Radiomóvil Dipsa, S.A. de C.V.; Renta de Equipo, S.A. de C.V.; Sercotel, S.A. de C.V.; Servicios y Supervisión, S.A. de C.V.; Teleconstructora, S.A.; and Teléfonos del Noroeste, S.A. de C.V.

The interest of foreign investors in TELMEX was not misplaced. Only three months after its privatization, the company showed impressive profits. According to a report released in April 1991, TELMEX profits for the first quarter of that year amounted to US$467 million. This translates into an annual profit of almost US$2 billion. Incomes in the first quarter of 1991 were 36 percent higher than for the same period of the previous year, with most revenue coming from local and long-distance calls. The new owners also benefited financially from a rise in the value of TELMEX shares. By March 15, 1991, AA shares had gone up on the New York stock market by US$0.10.[14] The increase created a profit of US$88.9 million for the new owners.[15] Based on these financial considerations the company is planning to invest approximately US$10 billion in network upgrading and expansion during the first half of the 1990s.

The second stage of the TELMEX privatization was also a success for the Salinas administration. By mid-June 1991 the government had sold L-type shares, representing 16.5 percent of the company, on foreign stock markets for US$2.27 billion.[16] Mexico sold 1.745 million L-type shares, which were offered on stock markets all over the world in the form of American Depository Shares (ADSs) at US$27.25 for each ADS.[17] Telephone workers and the controlling consortium also purchased TELMEX shares. The union, using a credit of US$325 million from the Mexican government, bought 187 million type A shares through Nacional Financiera, which constitutes 4.4 percent of TELMEX's capital. Carso Group, Southwestern Bell, and France Cable et Radio had access to 5.1 percent of the capital through type L shares. In this way, Southwestern Bell, for example, will buy US$467.3 million worth of L shares, doubling its participation in TELMEX. Table 5.1 shows the ownership distribution of the privatized 55.9 percent of TELMEX. The acquisition of TELMEX shares by local and foreign investors has made the sale of the telephone company the fourth largest privatization in the world.

The presence of prestigious foreign telecommunications companies in the management and ownership of TELMEX, as well as the success of the international sale of TELMEX shares, has sharply increased the value of the company. According to Dr. Pedro Aspe Armella, Mexico's secretary of finance and public credit, the capital worth of the Mexican telephone company in 1991 was approximately US$14.4 billion, which represents an increase in value of twelve times since TELMEX's privatization.[18]

Table 5.1   Share Distribution of TELMEX, September 1991

Owner	Share type	Percentage	Approximate value (million US$)
Carso Group	AA	10.4	860
Southwestern Bell	AA	5.0	425
France Cable et Radio	AA	5.0	425
Carso Group, Southwestern Bell, and France Cable et Radio	L	5.1	701
TELMEX union	A	4.4	325
Foreign investors (from U.S., Canada, Japan, Germany, France, U.K., Switzerland, and others)	L	16.5	2,270
Mexican government	L	9.5	1,307
Total	AA, A, L	55.9	6,313

Source: Author, based on various sources.

Other services in the Latin American telecommunications market have also entered a period of sharp reform. Cellular telephony, like any other emerging telecommunications technology, would have been a state-owned service in a preprivatization scenario. Today, however, the progressive liberalization and privatization of telecommunications services have turned Latin American governments into astonished witnesses of an international battle among companies of all origins to provide basic and enhanced telecommunications services. The large-scale competition of foreign companies for the concessions of Mexican regional cellular networks shows the attractiveness of the market and the growing confidence of high-tech foreign companies in the Latin American communications business. When the Mexican Secretariat of Communications and Transport opened the bidding for the provision of cellular services with the requirement of a minimum of US$1.5 million of capital and proven technical expertise, it never expected that 106 applications fulfilling all the requirements would be submitted to compete for the eight regional concessions that the government was granting. Table 5.2 shows how the eight concessions were granted.

Local cellular telephony is not the only area of enhanced telecommunications services in which foreign involvement is visible. Some foreign companies, such as Princeton Consulting, Inc., and Satellite Applications

TABLE 5.2   Regional Cellular Telephone Concessions Awarded in Mexico, 1991

Region	Company	Owners
1. Baja California Norte	Baja Celular Mexicana	Tecelmex
Baja California Sur	General Cellular Co.	Local investors
2. Sonora, Sinaloa	Movitel del Noroeste, S.A.	McCaw
		Cellular Comm.
		Contel Cellular Inc.
		Local investors
3. Chihuahua, Durango, and Torreón	Telefonía Celular del Norte	Domos International
	Motorola	Centel Cellular Co.
		Local investors
4. Nuevo León, Tamulipas, and Coahuila	Celular de Telefonía	Millicom Inc.
		Local investors
5. Jalisco, Colima, and Michoacan	Comunicaciones Celulares de Occidente, S.A.	Racal Inc.
		BellSouth
		Local investors
6. Aguascalientes, S.L.P., Zacatecas, Guanajuato, Querétaro, and various cities and towns	Sistemas Telefónicos Portátiles Celulares, S.A.	Bell Canada
		Local investors
7. Puebla, Tlaxcala, Veracruz, Oaxaca, and Guerrero	Telecomunicaciones del Golfo, S.A.	Bell Canada
		Local investors
8. Chiapas, Tabasco, Yucatán, Campeche, and Quintana Roo	Portatel del Sureste, S.A.	Associated Communic.
	LCC Co.	Local investors
Regions 1, 4, and 5 above	Radiomóvil Dipsa[a]	Southwestern Bell
		France Cable et Radio
		Carso Group (local)

a. Radiomóvil Dipsa is a subsidiary of TELMEX that was granted concessions in certain regions of the country because of high demand for cellular services.
SOURCE: "Situación Actual y Perspectivas de las Telecomunicaciones en México," *Proyecto de Asistencia Preparatoria* (Mexico City: Instituto Mexicano de Comunicaciones, 1991).

Engineering Corporation, have applied for government licenses to install satellite mobile systems. Further, some companies are taking advantage of technological innovations and the acceptance by less-developed countries of the "nonresidence" principle.[19] Such is the case of Overseas Telecommunications, Inc. and Houston International Teleport, which compete with the SIT Group of Mexico City to provide international high-speed data services through the Morelos satellite systems. From Ciudad Juárez, Sersa/Geocom, Inc., offers a satellite-based telecommunications service throughout the northern border area of Mexico. This is just a sample of cases from a growing market that was traditionally under government control and is now opening to private foreign and domestic participation. Mexican officials expect in the short term a quick diversification of communications services in the country, which they believe will be supported by a strong presence of foreign capital.

Airlines, banks, and other economic sectors

Beyond telecommunications, airlines and related services represent the second most important sale involving foreign capital by the Salinas administration. On August 22, 1989, Compañía Mexicana de Aviación, S.A. de C.V., the largest state-owned airline, was sold to the XABRE Group.[20] The consortium is formed by The Chase Manhattan Bank, N.A.; DBL Americas Development Association, L.P.; and G.O. (III) Ltd.[21] In the same deal the government sold to the XABRE Group two other state-owned enterprises related to the airline business: Aeropuertos y Terrenos, S.A., and Datatronic, S.A. The state keeps a minority share in both companies. XABRE gained control over the Mexicana de Aviación group of companies, which today is named Corporación Mexicana de Aviación, S.A. de C.V., contributing to a capital increase of US$140 million and comprising US$3 billion of investments in the next ten years.[22] The amount received by the government was reinvested in the company for modernization and development purposes.

Under the 1989 investment regulations the government planned to keep banking under state control, yet this provision was revised in 1990 when the Mexican congress passed regulations approving the reprivatization of commercial banks. According to the new legal framework, foreign investors may own up to 30 percent of the controlling stock of Mexican banks, while individual foreign bidders may acquire no more than 5 percent of the controlling shares.

Despite this opening to foreign direct investment, the first seven banks that were transferred to the private sector were all bought by Mexican nationals.[23] Further, in late 1991 there was no clear sense as to whether foreign investors would participate significantly in the sale of the other eleven banks that were still waiting to be reprivatized.[24]

In the oil industry, it is fairly clear that PEMEX (Petróleos Mexicanos) will not be privatized. In August 1989, however, the government carried forward a deep conceptual restructuring of the petroleum sector, reducing state participation and dominance. The traditional criteria for basic petrochemicals were redefined, and fourteen "basic" petrochemicals were reclassified as "secondary," leaving the number of basic items at twenty. At the same time, the list of secondary items was reduced from eight hundred to sixty-six. As a result of these reforms, extensive sectors of petrochemical production have been opened to private foreign participation.

The opening of industrial sectors involves areas such as the chemical and shipping industries. The presence of Japanese and Norwegian companies in these industries is an example of the diverse origins of foreign investment in the Mexican privatization program. On May 30, 1990, Fermentaciones Mexicanas, S.A. de C.V., was partially sold to a Japanese consortium formed by Kiowa Hakko Kogyo Co., Ltd., and Sumitomo Co. for US$16 million, with the state keeping a minority share. Eight months later, on January 31, 1991, a Norwegian group, Sokana Industries, Ltd., bought Astilleros Unidos de Veracruz, S.A. de C.V., for US$18.5 million, becoming the sole owner.[25]

In late 1991 the government was preparing a second round of privatization in which foreigners will play a still more important role. In late 1991 and early 1992, Salinas and his privatization team planned to offer several state-owned enterprises through public auction, in some of which foreign participation is allowed up to 100 percent. In this regard, the most interesting case is the steel conglomerate, of which Siderúrgica de México, S.A. de C.V. (SIDERMEX), Altos Hornos de México, S.A., and Siderúrgica Lázaro Cárdenas Las Truchas, S.A., are the main companies.[26] According to *The Economist*, the Mexican government could obtain up to US$2 billion dollars in revenues through the privatization of this steel conglomerate.[27] At the same time the government will offer in public auction Constructora de Carros de Ferrocarril, with 100 percent foreign ownership allowed; Aseguradora Mexicana, which allows 49 percent foreign ownership; and Sociedades Nacionales de Crédito, where foreign ownership of up to 30 percent of the controlling shares is permitted.

According to a state report, privatization has allowed the Mexican state to reallocate resources more productively and to concentrate on the provision of public services in areas of basic needs. The state is becoming a smaller and more efficient institution in the management of Mexico's modernization strategy and the insertion of the country in the global economy.[28] What is not yet clear, however, is what will be the effect of privatization on the economy as a whole and how the recently sold state-owned enterprises will perform.

Argentina

Following a path similar to that taken by Mexico, Argentina enjoyed moderate growth during the 1970s. Like most countries in the region, however, Argentina entered a period of deep crisis in the early 1980s, and its economy slid into a long period of recession and negative growth. In response to the regressive trend of the economy, policy makers began to consider structural reforms. By the mid-1980s the government was ready to carry forward, despite strong political opposition, profound changes in the country's economic guidelines. A key factor in this transformation was the restructuring of the state and the strengthening of the private sector, including the immediate privatization of numerous state-owned enterprises.

The first steps toward implementing a privatization program began during the Alfonsín administration in the mid-1980s. During these years a few minor businesses were sold to domestic entrepreneurs. The largest state-owned enterprises were not privatized until the following government administration. What is interesting about the early privatization program is that from the very beginning foreign direct investment was targeted as a priority. The most serious efforts to sell two of the major state-owned enterprises (ENTEL and Aerolíneas Argentinas) were intended to entice foreign capital into the country. Minister of Public Works and Services Rodolfo Terragno reached agreements with Telefónica from Spain (a prospective buyer of Empresa Nacional de Telecomunicaciones, or ENTEL)[29] and the Swedish airline company SAS (a prospective buyer of Aerolíneas Argentinas). The project failed because of Peronist opposition in congress.[30]

A few months later, however, when the Peronist candidate won the May 1989 presidential elections, privatization projects were immediately revived. The privatization program implemented was so radical that Argentina became, in a short time, the leading force in state reform in Latin America. President Carlos Menem's project included, in the short run, major state companies such as ENTEL (telecommunications), Aerolíneas Argentinas (airlines), and Ferrocarriles Argentinos (railways). Foreign direct investment was a key element in the new privatization program. The case of ENTEL probably demonstrates this strong commitment to attract foreign capital most clearly.

Telecommunications

The Argentine telecommunications system was one of the few in the world that was, in the preprivatization period, a public-private duopoly. Although the state-run Empresa Nacional de Telecomunicaciones (ENTEL) controlled most of the telephone lines throughout the country, six provinces had been served since 1927 by Compañía Argentina de Teléfonos (CAT), a private company that is a subsidiary of Erickson, a Swedish telecommunications corporation.[31]

For privatization purposes ENTEL was split into two new companies, Telco Norte and Telco Sur.[32] For operational purposes the country was also divided into two regions, north and south. Each company would be granted a monopoly for the provision of services in its corresponding area. After this structural change, ENTEL was put up for sale under two main conditions that involved foreign participation. First, the future managers, who would control 60 percent of ENTEL's stock, should be foreign common carriers with proven expertise in the field.[33] The government believed that no Argentine company had the technical or managerial expertise necessary to upgrade the Argentine telecommunications system as was required. Second, in exchange for 60 percent of ENTEL's shares, buyers were required to supply a maximum of US$214 million in cash, US$380 million in Argentine foreign debt payable over a three-year period, plus the maximum amount of debt papers that each consortium could offer, with a floor of US$3.5 billion.[34] This was the result of a long official debate on whether Argentina should try to get cash for the company or should follow the international bankers' criteria and erase part of its foreign debt through a debt-equity swap mechanism.[35] Because the latter method was chosen, bidders for ENTEL were inevitably foreign consortia, each consisting of a foreign international bank (the owners of debt papers) and a foreign common carrier (the owners of the technical expertise). Local companies entered the groups as financial partners, mainly for their lobbying capacity and knowledge of the domestic market.

Various foreign common carriers, including GTE, BellSouth, Nynex International, Bell Atlantic, Continental Telephone (United States), STET (Italy), Telefónica (Spain), Cable & Wireless (England), France Cable et Radio (France), and Siemens (Germany), showed interest in investing in the Argentine telecommunications sector. The finalists were three consortia, in each case headed by a foreign telephone company and a foreign bank; Bell Atlantic and Manufacturers Hanover; Telefónica and Citicorp; and STET (with France Cable et Radio) and J. P. Morgan. The winning consortium was STET–France Cable et Radio for the north region and Telefónica for the south. Each consortium will control 60 percent of the new companies, while the remaining 40 percent will be divided between ENTEL workers (10 percent) and the national and international stock markets (30 percent).

The sale brought the state US$214 million in cash (US$114 million for the south, and US$100 for the northern region), US$380 million in notes (US$203 million for the southern region, and US$177 million for the north), and US$4.95 billion in debt papers (TELECOM paid US$1.86 billion in public debt and US$372 million in accrued interest, and Telefónica paid US$2.18 billion in public debt and US$540 in accumulated interest). Yet, if we take the value of the debt papers in the secondary market at the time of the sale (which was approximately 11 cents on the dollar), the price paid for the company drops to US$1.5 billion.

Table 5.3 shows the composition of the STET consortium that owns Telco Norte, now called TELECOM. Table 5.4 shows the composition of Compañía de Inversiones en Telecomunicaciones (COINTEL), which bought Telco Sur and which operates today under the name of Telefónica de Argentina.[36]

After the purchase of ENTEL south by the Telefónica consortium, the participation and diversification of foreign capital quickly expanded. The company offered preferred shares in the international stock market, through Citicorp, which were bought by various foreign corporations. Table 5.5 shows the distribution of the offered shares.

Although they operate separate monopolies in the north and south of Argentina, TELECOM and Telefónica are partners in the provision of international services through TELEINTAR, and they share also the control of STARTEL, a recently created company that provides enhanced

TABLE 5.3   Distribution of Shares in TELECOM, Argentina, 1990

Company	Percentage of shares
France Cable et Radio[a]	44.25
STET[b]	44.25
Compañía Naviera Pérez Companc[c]	6.50
J. P. Morgan Bank	5.00

a. France Cable et Radio is the international branch of the state-owned France Telecom, a powerful telecommunications conglomerate that provides monopoly services throughout France. The company also controls ALCATEL, which is one of the main providers of telecommunications equipment in the Argentine market.
b. STET, Società Finanziaria Telefonica, is part of the Italian Institute for Industrial Reconstruction. The telecommunications holding company controls a variety of other enterprises related to the sector such as SIP, Italcable, Telespazio, Italtel, Sirti, Aet, Necsy, Siemens Data, and Cselt. The company also has indirect participation in Sic, Consultel, Accesa, Seva, SIRM, Telesoft, SSGRR, Data Spazio, and Teleo.
c. Compañía Naviera Pérez Companc, one of Argentina's most powerful economic groups, has a considerable share in Pecomnec, an Argentine-Japanese telecommunications equipment producer that had a close commercial relationship with ENTEL.
SOURCE: Secretariat of Planning, Argentina.

TABLE 5.4   Distribution of Shares in Telefónica de Argentina, 1990

Company	Percentage of shares
Citicorp Venture Capital	20.00
Banco Río (Cayman)	14.56
Telefónica International Holding[a]	10.00
Techint[b]	8.31
Banco Central, S.A. (Spain)	7.04
Comercial del Plata	5.00
Banco Hispano Americano	5.00
Manufacturers Hanover	4.33
Bank of Tokyo	4.16
Bank of New York	4.16
Zurich Ltd.	4.16
APDT	4.03
Arab Banking Co.	3.41
Republic New York Finanziaria	1.50
Centrobanco (Panama)	1.42
Vanegas Ltd.	1.25
Banco Atlantico, S.A.	0.75
Bank of Nova Scotia	0.60
BFG	0.30

a. Telefónica International Holding, the telecommunications operator of COINTEL, is a society of private law, with the minority participation (34.1 percent) of the Spanish government, a distributed share among foreign investors (22 percent), and domestic capital (43.9 percent).
b. Techint is an Italian multinational that provides telecommunications construction services (among many other commercial activities). It also has much experience in the Argentine market.
SOURCE: Telefónica de Argentina.

telecommunications services. Enhanced (or value added) services is the only sector of the Argentine telecommunications business in which market forces were unleashed and providers must operate in a relatively open and competitive environment.

Of ENTEL's remaining shares (defined as *ENTEL residual*), 10 percent is being reserved for the telephone employees and 30 percent was sold, starting in late 1991, on the national and international stock markets. A group of banks was in charge of the operation. Banco Roberts was the main advisor and manager of the sale, while Banco de Galicia, Banco Río, Banco del Sud, and Banco Crédit Lyonnais managed the sale to private investors. Because of the state's need for capital, the banks deposited in advance US$300 million in official accounts.[37] The government earned US$2 billion with this operation.

ENTEL's privatization considerably increased foreign direct investment in the Argentine telecommunications market, though foreign capital was already present in the early diversification of the industry, as in the development of cellular telephony and data services. In early 1988 the

TABLE 5.5   Distribution of Preferred Shares of Telefónica de Argentina, 1991

Company	Percentage of shares
APDT	24.1
Manufacturers Hanover	15.5
Bank of Tokyo	9.6
Union Bank of Switzerland	6.1
West LB International	5.4
First National Bank of Boston	5.1
Select Arcturus Holding	4.2
Generale Bank	4.0
Riobank Inter, Trust	3.9
Bank Fuer G.A.	2.9
Westdeutsche L.G.	2.9
Société Generale Panama	2.7
Swiss Bank Corporation	2.6
DG Bank Deutsche G.	1.7
Midland Bank PLC	1.7
Deutsche-Sudamericanische	1.3
Dresdner Bank A.	1.3
Banco Hispano Americano	1.1
N.V. Philips G.	1.1
Bank of Nova Scotia	1.0
Caterpillar Americas Co.	0.7
R N B and Co.	0.7
Republic New York Finanziaria	0.4

Source: Telefónica de Argentina.

government opened to private investment the concession of cellular telephone services in the Buenos Aires area. By July of the same year a consortium led by BellSouth won the public bidding and was granted the license to operate what the following year came to be the first private cellular network in Latin America. The consortium, which has strong foreign participation and operates under the commercial name of Movicom, comprises BellSouth (31 percent), Motorola (25 percent), Citicorp (8 percent), and two local companies—Socma (16 percent) and BGH (20 percent). The government also plans to offer to private investors concessions of cellular systems throughout the country. Based on the massive competition for the Mexican cellular system, Argentina expected strong interest in these offers.

In data and enhanced services, a fast-growing telecommunications sector, foreign financial companies are becoming partners of local entrepreneurs or installing their own services.[38] The government granted concessions to five companies besides STARTEL (owned by the new owners of ENTEL) to operate data transmission at the domestic level.

IMPSAT, SATELNET, and recently ALCATEL are the active ones; the other two companies (Keydata and TECSEL) hold licenses to operate but are presently out of the market. Among the active companies, SATELNET is a good example of joint venture trends with foreign capital participation. The company, originally owned by a local group, includes today the participation of the Italian financial group Banca Nazionale del Lavoro. Other telecommunications services, such as electronic mail, are carried out in Argentina through U.S. companies such as Sprint Mail and MCI Mail.

Airlines, railways, and tourism

By Presidential Decree 1591/89, the Argentine government offered for sale the national air carrier Aerolíneas Argentinas and its related companies, Buenos Aires Catering, S.A., and Operadora de Servicios Turísticos, S.A. (OPTAR). This was a partial privatization of the enterprise, in which the state retained 5 percent of the shares with a voting veto on issues related to defense and national security. Employees of the company held 10 percent of stock shares; foreign investors could hold no more than 50 percent. The remaining 35 percent was reserved for domestic private entrepreneurs. A peculiar requirement for the sale was that the principal buyer had to be a foreign airline with greater operational capacity than Aerolíneas Argentinas and could not hold more than 30 percent of the offered shares.

The only bid offered was by the Spanish airline Iberia in a consortium with local companies. Aerolíneas Argentinas was sold on November 21, 1990, to the group for US$130 million in cash, US$130 million over a ten-year period, and US$2.01 billion in foreign debt. The new owners committed to an investment of US$684 million in the first five years. After the sale the consortium was restructured. Today the group comprises Iberia Líneas Aéreas de España, S.A. (30 percent); a Spanish investment group (19 percent); Amadeo Riva (17 percent); Devi Construcciones, S.A. (17 percent); and a local group (2 percent).

Railway operations and assets are also for sale. Although passenger transportation is reserved for Argentine investors, cargo transportation is open to both foreign and local private parties. The first railway was sold on April 15, 1991, to a group comprising the Italian company Techint, U.S.-based Iowa Interstate Railroad, Chase Manhattan Investment, and several domestic groups. Techint, the leader of the group, holds 58 percent of the stock shares, while all other participants control 22 percent. The remaining shares are already in the hands of local private investors (16 percent) and railway workers (4 percent). The contract gave a thirty-year cargo concession to operate the Delta-Rosario-Bahía Blanca route (3,250 miles), for which the group paid the state US$155 million.

Four other cargo transport routes were offered, and four interested consortiums submitted bids for them in 1991. Two of the groups are interested in acquiring the Ferrocarril Mitre concession (3,125 miles). The first comprises Montana Rail Link, Banco Francés del Río de la Plata, and local partners; the second, Interamerican Railways Corporation, Sideco Americana, and local investors. The San Martin railway route (3,375 miles) has attracted the attention of a group including Railroad Development Corporation, Transapelt, and local companies. A group headed by Canadian International (a subsidiary of Canadian National Railways), NMB Post Bank Group (Holland), and domestic investors is trying to buy the shorter route of Ferrocarril Belgrano (441 miles). Finally, the government is about to sign a contract to transfer Ferrocarril Urquiza to a consortium headed by the Spanish railway company Renfe.

President Menem also included the state-run metro system, Subterráneos de Buenos Aires, in the list of state-owned enterprises to be sold during 1991–1992. The system, scheduled to be in private hands by the end of 1992, comprises five lines extending thirty miles and transporting 140 million passengers a year. Various European companies (including Transytem/Fiat, Ansaldo Transporti, Intermetro, Breda Ferroviaria, Valente, Matra, London Transport, and some Spanish companies) were interested in the metro sale.

In the tourism business, one of the most important privatizations including foreign participation was the sale of the famous Hotel Llao-Llao. Constructed in the internationally renowned area of Bariloche, the hotel was bought by the Citicorp-Choice-Cofipa-Surhotel group, which paid US$6.24 million for the tourist complex. The sale was completed with the requirement that new investment be made before the reopening of the complex.

Oil and steelworks

The project to privatize Yacimientos Petrolíferos Fiscales (YPF) was officially announced in 1987 by the Alfonsín administration. Since then, other than the licensing of oil exploration and production concessions, no major steps have been taken to transfer this huge oil enterprise to the private sector. The company, which is the fourth largest business in Latin America, has borderline public support for privatization.[39] Political issues concerning the size of the business, the sovereignty implications of oil control, a strong union, and political party oppositions have delayed any attempts to put it up for sale.[40]

Menem, however, turned a deaf ear to such politically sensitive matters, appointing as the head of YPF a businessman who, for many years, headed the Argentine branch of the U.S. oil company Hughes Tool

Co. The goal of the new YPF president is to transform the company into a semiprivate enterprise within a few months. In 1991 the federal government controlled the majority of shares in YFP, while provincial governments with oil operations in their territories owned the remainder. The plan is to sell to private investors 45 percent of the stock, with the federal government retaining 27.5 percent; governments of oil-producing provinces, 17.5 percent; and YPF workers, 10 percent. After the announcement of YPF privatization, in August of 1991, foreign oil companies Shell, Esso, Texaco, and ELF expressed interest in YPF shares.

Parallel to the YPF privatization project, government officials restructured and opened to private investment the exploitation of some of the country's richest oil fields. This process, which started with Alfonsín (under the label of the Houston plan), reached its zenith in 1990–1991. In the four richest oil fields (called *áreas centrales*), YPF signed joint ventures with private firms from France, Spain, and the United States to share 50 percent of the exploitation of oil resources.[41] These concessions have provided the government an income of US$600 million. In secondary areas (*áreas secundarias*), twenty-eight concession contracts have been granted for a total of US$252 million, nine more areas have been licensed, and another twenty-eight are scheduled to be offered in the early 1990s. For the latter, the government expects to collect US$100 million. Some of the foreign oil companies that were granted concessions in these areas are Amoco, Chevron, Braspetro (Brazil), British Gas, Exxon, Marathon, BHP Petroleum Pry, Occidental, Repsol (Spain), Shell, Total (France), Trend Exploration, and Triton Energy. The U.S.-based oil company Texaco, which had ceased all operations in Argentina thirty-six years before, has invested more in Argentina's oil industry since 1989 than any other foreign corporation.

In steelworks, privatization programs have been moving slowly. On the conviction that private presence is required in this sector, President Menem recently appointed a new head of the largest state-run steelworks (SOMISA), with a clear mandate to sell the company in the next few months. Four international consulting firms (McKinsey, Booz Allen & Hamilton, Rolan Berger, and Braxton) bid for the first stage of privatization, a study of the status of the company. The selection of Braxton as the official consulting firm moved the process forward, and the government is expecting purchase offers from Brazil, Japan, and Italy (including Techint).

Electricity, gas, and water

Public services such as electricity, gas, and water are also in the process of being privatized. In June 1991 the government signed a contract with the Canadian consulting firm Hydro Quebec to propose guidelines for the sale of Servicios Eléctricos del Gran Buenos Aires (SEGBA). During the same month C.S. First Boston Inc., Kleinwort and Benson Ltd., and Banco

General de Negocios were selected to manage the financial operation. SEGBA was transferred to its new owners in May 1992. Gas del Estado and Obras Sanitarias are at a similar stage as SEGBA; these companies are also scheduled to pass into private hands in the near future. The government has had talks with interested bidders such as Deutsche Bank (Germany).

Privatization of state-owned enterprises in Argentina has attracted, through various financial mechanisms, a considerable amount of foreign direct investment. The prospect of further foreign capital inflows improves as the privatization program is consolidated and the country's economy becomes more stable and prosperous. Besides some economic problems tied to foreign direct investment, Argentina is expecting approximately US$700 million of additional investments in the privatized sectors.[42] The same concerns that exist in Mexico, regarding the future performance of privatized companies and the effect of privatization on the economy of the country, are also germane to Argentina, however.

Chile

The reform of the state sector in Chile began in 1974 under the administration of General Augusto Pinochet, making it the earliest privatization program carried out in Latin America. The process can be divided into two clearly defined stages: the first, from 1974 to 1978, and the second, from 1985 to the present.

In the early 1970s, during the government of President Salvador Allende, the number of state enterprises grew dramatically in keeping with Allende's socialist philosophy. The number of companies run by the state grew from 64 in 1970 to 498 by the end of the Allende administration three years later. In reaction to this socialization of the Chilean economy, the authoritarian government of General Pinochet emphasized the reprivatization of state-owned enterprises. During the first months of the program 250 companies were returned gratis to their previous owners, and in the following years, 232 companies were sold to the private sector.[43] By 1980 the state controlled only 43 enterprises.[44]

Despite these impressive figures, the first phase of privatization was not a very rewarding experience for Chile. The deep national economic crisis of 1982 drove many of these privatized businesses to bankruptcy, and once more there were calls for state intervention. The government had to take over and start running sixteen of the main financial institutions and a number of commercial and industrial companies such as COPEC, INDUS, INFORSA, Celulosa Arauco, and Celulosa Constitución.[45] By 1984–1985 the economy began to show signs of recovery, a fact that immediately led the neoliberal Pinochet economic team to start a second round of privatization.

From 1985 on, the government not only privatized more than forty state-owned enterprises; it also achieved a considerable increase in foreign direct investment. By the end of 1989 there was extensive foreign participation in such privatized state-owned enterprises as CAP (steel), CTC (telecommunications), CHILGENER (electricity), ENAEX (explosives), IANSA (sugar), Lab Chile (laboratories), LAN-Chile (airlines), PILMAIQUEN (electricity), and SOQUIMICH (chemicals and minerals). Two of these companies (CTC and LAN-Chile) not only represent an important part of foreign direct investment in Chile, but also show an interesting dynamic created by the presence of foreign companies, and are therefore worth describing in some detail.

Telecommunications

Telephone services in Chile date as far back as 1880, with the creation of the Compañía de Teléfonos de Edison in Valparaíso. From 1927 to 1974 telecommunications services in the country were controlled by the International Telephone and Telegraph Corporation (ITT). In 1974 the Chilean government acquired 80 percent of the Compañía de Teléfonos de Chile (CTC). Between that date and the time of its privatization, despite the government's majority shareholdings, the company was subject to private law jurisdiction.

CTC's privatization is no doubt the most significant in Chile. CTC, which is the largest telecommunications company in the country, provides local telephone service to 77 percent of the national territory and owns 94 percent of all phone lines in Chile. In 1990 CTC had 867,076 lines installed, and the company plans to reach US$1.4 billion of new investments by the end of the 1988–1992 period.

In August 1987, CORFO (the government holding company and development bank that held 80 percent of CTC's stock shares) announced the sale of 151 million common shares, series A, which accounted for approximately 30 percent of the government share in the company. By January 1988 CORFO transferred the shares to Bond Corporation Chile, S.A., which offered the highest price: US$114.8 million.[46] Throughout 1988 Bond Corporation increased its participation in CTC capital stock, buying shares in various other offerings. By the end of the year, and after investing US$285 million, Bond was in control of 50 percent of CTC's subscribed capital stock.[47]

The managerial skill and the financial eagerness of Bond turned the company around in a short time. By 1989 CTC was transformed from a slow-moving parastatal enterprise into a fast-growing business with a fresh image and an impressive presence in the market. The new private owners found ways to raise funds to upgrade and expand the network. The corporation got financing from equipment providers, from future customers, and from the sale of shares on the local and international stock markets. The sale of CTC's shares on the New York Stock Exchange was probably the most beneficial inheritance that would be left to the company by the short-lived Bond ownership. Profits increased to US$100 million a year, and 100 percent of profits was paid through dividends to shareholders. Two years later, however, the international Bond empire collapsed, and Bond's business in Chile suffered the consequences. CTC was sold in April 1991 to Telefónica de España for US$392 million. Alan Bond not only made a profit of US$100 million a year during the time he operated the company, but also made a profit of approximately US$100 million on the sale operation.

The purchase of CTC's controlling share by Telefónica created jurisdictional problems, however, because the Spanish company also has a considerable share in ENTEL (the Chilean long-distance telephone company). The Spanish common carrier acquired 20 percent of ENTEL's shares in an early privatization of the company. Additionally, Telefónica's official bank, the Bank of Santander, controls 10 percent of ENTEL's voting shares. In this way, Telefónica not only has a strong regional presence, but also poses monopoly problems for the Chilean government.[48] The government's Preventive Commission ruled that Telefónica should keep its shares in only one company, selling its part in the other. But the Spanish entrepreneurs hope to keep a stake in both companies and have appealed the ruling, which must ultimately be resolved by the Chilean supreme court.

Besides foreign participation in local and long distance telephone services, Chile, like many other Latin American countries, has a considerable amount of foreign investment in its cellular telephone system. The market, which is growing fast, is divided among four companies: (1) CTC holds a license for nationwide services; (2) Cidcom de Telefonía Celular de Chile, owned by Pacific Telecom, holds licenses for Santiago and Valparaíso; (3) VTR Telecomunicaciones, owned by the British company Millicom and VTR Telecomunicaciones, holds a nationwide license that excludes Santiago; and (4) TELECOM, constituted by ENTEL-Chile (33.3 percent), Télex-Chile (33.3 percent), and Motorola (33.3 percent), also holds a nationwide license that excludes Santiago.

The Chilean telecommunications system already has a strong foreign presence, but as the country strives to become a player in the global economy, the need for high-tech telecommunications services will increase, demanding even greater participation by highly skilled companies from abroad.

Airlines

Privatization in Chile also had a considerable effect on the airline business. In early 1990 the government sold the national carrier, LAN-Chile, to the Scandinavian airline SAS, in a joint venture with local investors. The group paid US$48 million in cash for 78 percent of the company's assets and the control of the business. SAS played an important role in this process by helping local investors to obtain an international loan to buy their part of the company and allowed the local investors to take control of the presidency of the company. The Scandinavian airline, which participated in both the early and the most recent offerings of Aerolíneas Argentinas, has shown interest also in other Latin American airline privatizations. Further, in the context of a globalization project, the European company purchased 17 percent of Continental Airlines for approximately US$32 million, making it the major shareholder of the U.S.-based company.

SAS, however, overextended its financial capability to achieve this global expansion (which included the purchase of hotels and resorts) at the same time that LAN-Chile become a money-losing business (losing US$4.5 million in the first half-year of business), and the company plunged into the red (with a debt of US$20 million). Strained by these financial burdens (in addition to a US$5 million loss caused by the Persian Gulf war), the company broke its alliance with the Chilean investors and built a new coalition with CORFO (the government holding company, which had kept 22 percent of LAN's shares). At that time the Chilean government was planning to sell its part in the company, but the crisis delayed official plans. As a result of realignments within the business, CORFO took over the presidency of LAN-Chile, and now the state leads the business of the private sector. The Chilean government, nevertheless, still plans to sell its shares as soon as the airline regains financial and operational stability.

Despite suffering large-scale failure in its first privatization attempts, Chile has been able to carry forward with moderate success its second privatization program. The country, which is seen today as a model of stable economic policy, has been able to attract large numbers of foreign investors. In fact, the effort to bring in investment from abroad has been so successful that the government is now trying to restrain the entrance of more foreign capital because of the fear that excessive capital inflows will intensify the country's existing inflationary pressures.

Privatization in the Early Stages: Venezuela, Ecuador, and Bolivia

After Argentina, Chile, and Mexico, the next most serious privatizer in Latin America seems to be Venezuela. By September 1991 the country had already privatized three commercial banks and its airline, Venezolana Internacional de Aviación, S.A., (VIASA); had granted the concession of a cellular telephone band; and was in the advanced stages of privatization of the state-owned telephone company (Compañía Anónima Nacional de Teléfonos de Venezuela—CANTV).

In early 1991 the administration of Carlos Andrés Pérez announced an important achievement in its ambitious privatization and liberalization program.[49] A joint venture comprising foreign telecommunications companies (the U.S. firm BellSouth and British-based Racal Telecom) and a Venezuelan group (BBS, Comtel, and Bancor) won a cellular telephone concession with the offer of US$107 million. The new company, run under the name of Telcel, will provide services in all major cities of the country.[50] Private participation in the cellular telephony business is considered the first component of CANTV's privatization. The sale of the telephone company, which is scheduled for the last months of 1991, has already attracted the attention of various foreign common carriers, such as U.S. West, Southwestern Bell, Bell Atlantic, Nippon Telephone & Telegraph, GTE, France Telecom, Bell Canada, and AT&T. Considering the strong presence of foreign companies in the Caribbean telecommunications system, the Venezuelan government, which is trying to fetch US$2 billion for the telecommunications company, expects a successful sale of CANTV.[51]

The other important privatization, the airline company VIASA, also involves considerable foreign investment: 60 percent of the company was bought by a group comprising the Spanish airline Iberia and Venezuela's Banco Provincial for US$145.5 million. A month before the sale six foreign airline companies—Alitalia, British Airways, Swissair, Northwest, Iberia, and KLM—were bidding for VIASA. In the final round the government's Venezuelan Investment Fund (Fondo de Inversiones de Venezuela, the entity in charge of privatizing VIASA) had narrowed the choice to the Dutch firm KLM and the ultimate winner Iberia. The privatization aftermath leaves the company's shares distributed as follows: Iberia, 45 percent; Banco Provincial, 15 percent; VIASA employees, 20 percent; and the Venezuelan government, 20 percent.

Neither Bolivia nor Ecuador has yet carried out any major privatizations with significant foreign direct investment, yet both countries have embarked on joint venture projects with foreign companies for oil exploration and production. Bolivia has started to privatize various activities related to the oil sector using contracts commonly referred to as "improved recoveries." Several of these contracts were signed during 1990–1991. In March 1991, for example, Texaco and Sun Oil signed an exploration and production contract with the state-owned Yacimientos Petrolíferos Fiscales Bolivianos (YPFB). This is a prospective investment of approximately US$25 million over a seven-year period. Around the same time, Esso Exploration of Bolivia was granted a thirty-year exploration concession with an estimated investment of US$40 million.

Bolivia has moved well along in the privatization of its state-run airline,

Lloyd Aéreo Boliviano (LAB). The oldest airline in Latin America, LAB has been evaluated by the First Boston Corporation and has several prospective foreign buyers such as Varig, Iberia, Hapag-Lloyd, and a Japanese consortium. Bolivia also plans to expand its privatization program to include the national rail company.

Ecuador is carrying out a quasi-privatization program in oil exploration and production. An example of this is the contract signed in August 1991 between the Ecuadoran oil company Petroecuador and a foreign consortium headed by Conoco of the United States.[52] The deal comprised a twenty-year joint venture to explore and produce heavy and extra heavy crude from deposits in the Amazon basin. Despite Conoco's strong initial commitment to the project (the company invested US$100 million in oil exploration and planned to spend US$700 million on drilling operations, in addition to the construction of a new highway and 130 miles of oil pipeline), and to the surprise of Ecuadoran government officials, the North American company pulled out of the consortium two months after signing the contract. US Maxus has taken the place of Conoco and assumed operatorship of the project, which plans to produce 350,000 barrels a day by 1995. Other foreign companies such as Texaco and US Oryx also participate in Ecuadoran oil production. The government will soon award new drilling areas to Mobil and Arco; three new candidates for further exploration in the country are the United States's Occidental, France's ELF, and Ecuador's Triepol.[53]

The government is also seeking the participation of foreign capital in the expansion of the nation's electricity grid. According to Minister of Energy and Mines Donald Castillo, the country requires a basic investment of US$3.04 billion to update hydroelectric power generation, transmission, and distribution in an eight-year program. In May 1991 the Ecuadorean Congress passed legislation to stimulate private domestic and foreign participation in mining activities through fiscal and monetary incentives for private investors.

The Late Privatizers: Brazil and Uruguay

Several other Latin American countries are developing comprehensive privatization programs, although many of them are still in the early stages, and flows of foreign direct investment to these countries are very limited. Nevertheless, in the most advanced cases the presence of interested foreign groups is evident, and governments are anticipating considerable foreign participation. Brazil is one such case.

When Fernando Collor de Mello took office on March 15, 1990, as the first democratically elected president of Brazil, it seemed that the country would embark on a broad reform of the public sector. The leading force of this public restructuring project would be, as in other Latin American countries, the massive privatization of state-owned enterprises. In March 1990 Decree No. 99464 listed the first twelve state-owned enterprises that would be transferred in the following months to the private sector. Eighteen months later, however, the first companies had not yet been sold.[54]

The first state-run company scheduled for sale was the steelworks complex Usinas Siderúrgicas de Minas Gerais, S.A. (USIMINAS). The company, responsible for 40 percent of domestic steel production and valued at US$1.08 billion, was scheduled for public stock offerings by October 24, 1991. The project had important political opponents, however, such as the country's then–vice president, Itamar Franco. The government actually sold 75 percent of the company's shares, with 94 percent of these shares going to Brazilian companies and 5.9 percent to foreign firms. The remaining 25 percent is to be divided between the company's employees (10 percent) and the state's current foreign private partner, Nippon Steel (15 percent). The subsequent planned privatization involves the electrical mechanical repair company, the Companhia Electromecânica Celma. The firm, for which the government expects to obtain US$73 million, is already partially owned (13 percent) by the U.S. firm United Technologies. Both Nippon Steel and United Technologies will have priority status to purchase up to 40 percent of the controlling shares of the company.

According to Brazilian legislation, sales of capital stock of state-owned enterprises (included in the Brazilian Denationalization Program) to foreigners (individuals or entities) cannot exceed 40 percent of the controlling shares of the company.[55] In exceptional cases a higher percentage may be approved by congress. Although this seems to be a serious restriction on foreign participation, loopholes in the laws will allow foreign investors to acquire 100 percent of the controlling shares of some Brazilian state-owned enterprises. The federal constitution accepts as Brazilian any company constituted in Brazil, regardless of the origin of the capital. Accordingly, any foreign investor who constitutes a new company under Brazilian regulations acquires all the rights of any other Brazilian company. Some members of congress are trying to close these loopholes by introducing reforms in the constitution.

Concerning other restrictions on private participation, the constitution is quite clear and straightforward. Certain state operations, such as telecommunications and petroleum refining, are considered public monopolies and are therefore not subject to privatization. Other state entities such as Petróleo Brasileiro (PETROBRAS), Banco do Brasil, S.A., and Instituto de Resseguros do Brasil cannot be transferred to the private sector, either. The constitution, however, can always be changed.

In Uruguay the Chamber of Deputies on September 27, 1991, passed a bill to privatize the state-run telephone company Administración Nacional de Telecomunicaciones (ANTEL). With this privatization the government is attempting to attract foreign partners to double the company's current US$50 million annual investment in telecommunications infrastructure throughout the country in order to satisfy unmet service demands. Uruguay regulations allow up to 49 percent of foreign direct investment in the telecommunications sector. Telefónica de España, France-Telecom, STET (Italy), Nynex (U.S.), Bell Atlantic, and BellSouth have expressed interest.

What the Uruguayan government has already achieved in foreign direct investment in the telecommunications sector is the concession to a consortium of foreign and local investors of a radio spectrum band for the provision of cellular telephony. The group, composed of BellSouth, Abiatar, Motorola, and a domestic group, will operate in Montevideo and the southern coastal area.

Other Uruguayan enterprises likely to be privatized soon include Pluna (airlines), ILPE (fisheries institute), the national port authority, gas distribution, railways, UTE (electricity), OSE (water treatment and distribution), insurance, and alcohol distillation.

Late privatizers benefit from the experience of those countries that took the lead in state reform. The failures and successes of early cases will give latecomers knowledge and rich information in the most appropriate ways of selling state-owned enterprises. At the same time, however, these countries may find that, in a world market replete with privatizations, the available capital for purchasing state assets in developing countries may be more difficult to attract in large quantities by early offers, and the number of interested bidders may be sharply reduced, hampering the completion of privatization programs.

Assessing Foreign Direct Investment

Borrowing from the international financial community has been a sour experience for most Latin American countries. In the late 1970s extensive low-interest, long-term loans from international commercial banks gave countries in the region the illusion of easy access to large amounts of cheap capital. Governments felt that they were grabbing the appropriate tool for "autonomous" development. But the dream was short lived. By 1982 a steep increase in the interest rate of the accrued debt helped spur an unprecedented economic crisis, and most borrowers have since then had to confront serious economic constraints and a grim prospect for the years to come.

The high social and economic costs tied to foreign loans have left painful memories and serious questions regarding the previously unquestioned benefits of borrowing from abroad. Many politicians and techno-crats now in power are reconsidering the benefits of loans rather than foreign direct investment. As one Mexican government official believes, "it's better to have a partner than a creditor."[56] This very simple concept of how to engage foreign capital, plus the fact that loans from abroad have dropped off sharply in recent years, has again created a strong regional attraction to foreign direct investment.[57]

Renewed interest in foreign direct investment has also spurred a heated regional debate on the virtues and drawbacks of this particular form of foreign capital participation.[58] Based on the most relevant argu-ments raised in the framework of this debate, the following paragraphs will highlight the benefits offered and the problems created by the partici-pation of capital from abroad. The analysis will also include the effect of debt-equity swap privatizations on the local economy.

Advocates of foreign direct investment would argue that, because direct investments are a productive form of channeling capital resources into developing economies, foreign companies can contribute to the host economy with resources that are generally scarce in less-developed coun-tries. Compared with other modes of investment (such as international loans, which can be shifted to capital markets), foreign direct investment tends to favor the productive side of capital resources. The very nature of direct investment and the implicit capital risk that foreign participation implies lead nonfinancial foreign corporations to expand the productive capability of the business to its limits.

Businesses from abroad tend not only to bring new investment capital, but also to carry their own financing, relieving local governments of the burden of supporting credit lines for the sector. In the international context, multinational corporations today have better possibilities of devel-oping projects and gaining access to credits even in harsh economic environments.

Foreign companies can also play, through investment projects, an important role as a guarantor of new loans from the international credit market. An example of this potential advantage of foreign participation is offered by the privatization of the Chilean national airlines LAN-Chile. A local company that was interested in purchasing a share in the privatized airline was granted a loan of US$29 million by the Morgan Guaranty Trust Bank. The key to this transaction was the presence of the Scandinavian airline SAS as a partner of the Chilean company. SAS, which has been an important client of Morgan for a long time, provided the guarantee required by the bank.[59]

In regard to the transformation of the region's productive patterns, an increase in foreign direct investment may upgrade and enhance the tech-nological capability of the recipient country. Managerial experience in operating in international markets is another scarce resource that foreign businesses bring to Latin America. Decades of closed and protected economies have downgraded the managerial capacity and skill of Latin American entrepreneurs, a weakness that large multinationals can offset with their long-term international experience. The participation of multi-nationals, if guided by adequate trade policies, should also help to reverse the prevailing productive system of Latin America from an inward-led growth economy to an export-oriented economy. Large transnational corporations control worldwide commercial networks that would facilitate the access to markets abroad. It is the responsibility of domestic regulatory bodies to create incentives in this direction if the region intends to develop an export-oriented economy.

Supporters of foreign direct investment also argue that this type of investment has longer maturity periods than those developed by produc-tive and commercial cycles. Foreign direct investment slows down rather than reinforces the recessive patterns of the economic cycle. At the same time, foreign direct investment grants the benefit that profit remittances generally show a pro-cyclical dynamic that moves parallel to recessive tendencies. In other words, the remittance of foreign exchange abroad tends to increase when the economy is in expansion, and it tends to decrease when the economy confronts a period of recession.[60]

Governments of developing countries are also finding it easier to bargain with production-oriented companies rather than with interna-tional financial institutions. Two factors are central in the improvement of the bargaining position of developing countries. First, companies in the productive sector have specific productive and commercial interests and therefore tend to bargain on an individual basis. Commercial international banks tend to form strong cartels with which developing countries have very little chance of advancing their interests. Second, corporations are tied to fixed assets that must establish residence in the host country, while banks' operational resources (financial capital) have a volatile and elusive character.

On the other side of the debate, critics of foreign direct investment have stated that "multinational firms frequently do not bring in much, if any, new capital from outside when they invest. Rather, to establish themselves, they appropriate local capital for their own use, and they seek host country protection from competitive forces that might drive them to develop new, least-cost, labor-intensive production methods more appro-priate to a Third World locale."[61] From this point of view, foreign direct investment is explained as a global corporate strategy to set barriers to entry into certain industries and to extend worldwide the ability to extract rents.

Critics suggest that, although it is true that in recessive periods net profit remittance abroad tends to diminish, it is also true that, at least in Latin America's recent history, the general amount of foreign exchange sent abroad during those downward cycles does not decrease.[62] Frequently the experience of Latin America has been that during unstable and harsh economic times foreign direct investment follows the general behavioral pattern of other forms of investments, flowing abroad. Like private banks, multilateral institutions, and domestic private investors, multinational corporations tend to retreat from troubled countries at a quick pace, diverting capital resources to other regions of the world (see table 5.6).

Of particular interest among the various financial mechanisms under which governments have offered state-owned enterprises for sale are debt-equity swaps, because of the effect they have had on inducing foreign participation in Latin America's economy.[63] Compared with other forms of foreign direct investment, debt-equity swaps have in the past accounted for large inflows of foreign capital. In Chile, for example, in 1979–1986 regular foreign direct investment averaged US$205 million annually, while debt-equity swaps reached an average of US$400 million per year. In the case of Mexico in the same period, regular foreign direct investment amounted to US$932 million annually, while debt-equity swaps accounted for US$1,133 million of foreign participation.[64]

Studies by a World Bank team on debt-equity swaps and foreign direct investments in Latin America showed that swaps had a different effect on the willingness to invest of banks and multinational corporations. The study concluded that "virtually every investment made by banks would not have happened without a swap program." In the case of corporations, "about one-third of the investments made by MNCs [multinational corporations] would not have been made unless a swap program was available."[65]

For both banks and multinationals, swap programs carry extensive benefits. Banks can exchange poorly performing debt papers for tradeable

TABLE 5.6	Inflows of Direct Investment, 1970–1987 (annual average, in thousands of special drawing rights)			
	1970–1979	1980–1982	1983–1985	1986–1987
Latin America	2,031	5,347	3,503	3,577
North America	4,129	13,558	18,935	32,825
Western Europe	6,853	13,114	12,925	21,485
Japan	110	262	330	560
Southeast Asia	913	3,522	4,696	4,319
Other	2,495	9,223	8,233	5,373
Total	16,531	45,026	48,622	68,139

SOURCE: Inter-American Development Bank, *The World Economy, Latin America and the Role of the IDB* (Washington, D.C, 1989).

assets, an operation that increases the chances of liquidating part of the debt portfolios of less-developed countries sooner and under better conditions. Multinationals find swaps an excellent opportunity to invest at very low cost, buying debt shares in secondary markets at highly discounted prices.

For the host country, foreign direct investment through a privatization program can play an important role in supplementing investments, as it represents extra capital inflows that the government would have otherwise gotten from other sources. With the additional inflow of foreign capital, "the privatization policy will represent a genuine form of overcoming the restriction imposed by the rationing of external credit markets on investments."[66]

In most swap programs, however, the indebted country does not receive "fresh money," nor does it achieve an expansion of the country's productive system through "new investments." Debt-equity swaps have been used to buy existing state assets or companies, and they don't represent any "real" capital inflow.[67]

In the case of swaps, foreign direct investment becomes a temporary mechanism to finance the fiscal deficit, with a probable negative balance for the country in the long run.[68] In the early postprivatization period the country will enjoy the benefits of a considerable capital inflow, the reduction of debt services, and sectorial expansion due to required profit reinvestment.[69] These benefits are not likely to hold in the long term when nonresident companies began to remit net profits back to their home countries. In the face of a possible external squeeze (due to foreign exchange remittances), Latin American economists have recommended that foreign investments be directed to tradeable and exportable goods to reduce the possibility of an external sector imbalance in the future. Although the recommendation offers an attractive policy for privatization programs in the region, Latin American countries face the problem that most state-owned enterprises that are attractive to foreign investors are in the service sector. In the privatized services, therefore, "if the rate of return on physical capital is higher than the interest rate, the debt-equity swap mechanism could entail an increment in the balance of payments disequilibrium in the future."[70] Such is the preliminary result of a prospective study based on the case of ENTEL (see table 5.7).

The situation may deteriorate even further if the country does not develop an adequate regulatory body to oversee the company's profit growth. This is certainly so in industries such as telecommunications, where technological innovation, expanded economies of scale, and improvements in productivity rates tend to reduce costs and increase the business rate of return. The lack of a sensitive regulatory framework that would translate decreases in costs into lower tariffs would increase the

TABLE 5.7   External Effects of the Privatization of ENTEL, Argentina (Projected)

				Years following privatization					
	1	2	3	4	5	6	7	8	9	10
A. External public debt service payments saved[a] (million US$)	550	550	550	550	550	550	550	550	550	550
B. Flow of distributable dividends[b] (million US$)	250	150	230	430	330	400	600	700	900	900
B/A	0.45	0.27	0.42	0.78	0.60	0.73	1.09	1.27	1.63	1.63

a. This assumes that the 30 percent of ENTEL's shares that remain in the hands of the state are sold in exchange for debt papers.
b. Estimate based on ENTEL's having the same future level of efficiency performance as the Chilean telecommunications company and a low growth in message unit (pulso) use.
SOURCE: Pablo Gerchunoff and Lilian Castro, "La Racionalidad Macroeconómica de las Privatizaciones," mimeo (Buenos Aires: Instituto De Tella, August 1991), p. 17.

company's availability to remit foreign exchange abroad, to the detriment of domestic capital markets.

Furthermore, debt-equity swaps have, for the host country, an "over-payment" effect over the redeemed debt. Most countries are not fully servicing their debts, nor do they intend to do so.[71] Future payments for debt services are, therefore, expected to be lower than the amount at which the country redeems debt through swap operations.[72] Taking debt at its face value, the indebted country is unable to benefit from transactions at low prices in secondary markets.[73]

The operation has contradictory effects in that on one side it redeems debt, but on the other it turns poorly performing debt papers into a valuable financial instrument, raising their prices in secondary markets. Argentine debt papers, for example, were paid in secondary markets at 11 cents on the dollar at the moment of ENTEL's privatization.[74] After the government accepted more than US$5 billion (the largest debt-equity swap operation in Latin America) for the telephone company, the price of the Argentine debt started to rise, and by mid-1991 buyers were paying 23 cents on the dollar. Opponents of swap programs have also emphasized that these operations are carried out in a context of international discussions of debt relief that include the possibility of refinancing debt at its secondary market value.

These and other problems of debt-equity swap operations for host countries have created concerns not only in the academic world, but also in the political and economic spheres of less-developed countries. An example is the domestic opposition to the privatization of the Brazilian company USIMINAS. The company was originally scheduled to be sold September 24, 1991, with the government allowing the use of debt-equity swaps to purchase the company. The offering had to be postponed more than a month, however, because of a ruling by a lower federal court prohibiting the use of debt equity in the operation. The conflict between the federal government and federal jurists required the involvement of the Supreme Court, which ruled in favor of swap use for the USIMINAS sale.

It is true that these criticisms of debt-equity swap programs offer an "awareness guide" for Latin American policy makers. Nevertheless, it is also true that, for many state officials, policy making in the current historical context is an activity highly constrained by the critical economic conditions of their countries. The possibility of choosing alternatives to debt-equity swap programs has decreased as the crisis has expanded and become more overwhelming. For various governments in the region, swaps were the necessary condition to attract enough bidders to achieve a "successful" sale.

Attempts at privatization in Puerto Rico, Bolivia, and Argentina support this reasoning in regard to the unclear status of international privatization markets and the availability of disposable capital for would-be privatized enterprises. Puerto Rico had to cancel the sale of its telephone company because of the absence of bidders. Bolivia, despite the fact that it has offered a variety of state-owned enterprises in the international market, had not received any significant offers for any of its companies by late 1991. Argentina also had to cancel privatizations in the absence of interested buyers. By late 1991 numerous privatization programs active throughout the world had created a saturated market, in which vendors in risky or unattractive environments are in a weak position to determine the ideal conditions for the sale.[75]

Finally, the intense pressure exercised by the international financial community in favor of debt-equity swaps as the official mode of privatization has been, for many countries, the driving force in the decision-making process. To be able to offer state-owned enterprises to the private sector, various indebted Latin American governments had to require a "waiver" from their creditors, something that financial business leaders saw as an excellent opportunity to influence the conditions under which the operation would take place. Through debt-equity swaps, many international commercial banks were able to upgrade the performance of their depressed debt portfolios in Latin America, exchanging debt paper of questionable value for productive assets in developing economies.

Final Remarks

When several of the largest privatization projects were announced in mid-1989, Latin American policy makers were uncertain about the future success of the endeavor. Recent political and economic events in the world were diverting the attention of foreign and domestic investors to other areas of the globe, such as Eastern Europe, East and Southeast Asia, and various industrialized countries. Latin America in the late 1980s was not an attractive place for investors.

Governments have managed to change this bleak picture, however, and the region is recovering the position that it once had in the global distribution of capital resources. Privatization of state-owned enterprises seems to have been a key factor in this process, and a preliminary examination offers some evidence that programs in several countries have been quite successful in attracting foreign direct investment. During 1990 and 1991, just two countries (Argentina and Mexico) have, with the sale of their telephone companies, attracted the impressive amount of US$8.9 billion in investments. Argentina, Chile, and Mexico are today host countries to more than ninety foreign companies that participate directly or indirectly, through privatized enterprises, in the economic activities of these nations.

Certain governments have not only been successful in the sale of state-owned enterprises, but have also managed to control long-standing economic problems such as inflation, recession, and fiscal deficit. As the economy of the region becomes more stable and prosperous, the fate of privatization programs and the prospect for further foreign capital inflows might improve.

The future stability of foreign direct investment in Latin America is still quite uncertain, however. The privatization of some economic sectors has recently been shown to have unintended and undesirable consequences for the country's economic stability, a factor that will no doubt jeopardize the presence of foreign capital. The sale of Mexico's banking system to the domestic private sector is illustrative. In August of 1991, the Mexican government transferred to the private sector the first seven banks, part of what is planned to be the total reprivatization of the nation's banking system. The banks were bought by the same local groups that control the domestic stock market. At the time of the sale, Mexico enjoyed still weak, but growing economic stability and prosperity. Yet the financial operations implemented by these new private groups set in motion a spiral of financial speculations that spurred, for the first time in a long period, a transitory monetary crisis.[76]

In the view of some Mexican analysts, the government, by selling the banking system to a limited group of business interests related to the stock market, is leaving the control of the Mexican economy in those few hands. The speculative outlook of these business groups has already sparked what some observers define as a "casino economy." The monetary crisis prompted by the recently privatized banks was controlled by the Bank of Mexico, which flooded the financial market with 8 billion pesos (US$2.6 million), giving liquidity to the market and holding the speculative wave. There are fears that, with the banking system in the control of financial groups, the country's economy will return to instability and inflation.

The privatization of certain economic sectors will therefore require more and not less regulation. The stability and future credibility of current economic reforms call for a considerable degree of government intervention to guarantee that the new rules of the game are respected by domestic and foreign economic actors. This is even more true in the case of Latin America, where several years of inflation and economic instability have created a gambling mentality in those involved in productive activities.

Latin American countries have achieved a considerable success in the sale of state-owned enterprises and in attracting foreign direct investment to the recently privatized companies. Yet the future evolution of privatization in the region will very much depend on the success of stabilization programs and the reduction of political risks. For this reason, governments will have to keep close surveillance on the evolution of the domestic economy if they intend to invite foreign capital to participate in the region's journey toward progress.

Notes

1. Luis R. Luis, "Why Privatize in Latin America?" supplement to *Latin Finance* (March 1991), p. 6.

2. In countries like Argentina early attempts to privatize state-owned enterprises had little success. Only a few minor companies were transferred to the private sector. In most of Latin America during those years, rather than reducing its size and presence in the economy, the state expanded and became highly interventionist. See, for example, Horacio Boneo, ed., *Privatización: Del Dicho al Hecho* (Buenos Aires: El Cronista Comercial, 1985).

3. Argentina and Mexico, for example, showed an impressive growth of foreign investments in their stock exchange during the first months of 1991. In Mexico, foreign investments in the stock exchange grew 140 percent in the first five months of the year, while the Argentine capital market grew 291 percent in the first seven months of 1991. The month of August 1991 alone presented a historic boom in the country's stock exchange, with 650 percent growth over the previous month.

4. The cases were selected because of the large volume of foreign capital involved in the deal or because of the strategic value of the industry for its country. As common sense dictates, it is not the same to have foreign participation or control in the oil industry, telecommunications, or airlines as it is to have such involvement in forestry or leather or salt production unless the industry is of special strategic value in the country's economy, such as has been the case of copper in Chile.

5. Mexico, Secretariat for Commerce and Industrial Development, "Mexico and the Foreign Investor: A Partnership for Growth," mimeo (Mexico City, 1990). For extensive studies on Mexico's foreign direct investment, see Wilson Peres Núñez, *Foreign Direct Investment and Industrial Development in Mexico* (Paris: OECD Development Center, 1990), and Torben Huss, *FDI and Industrial Restructuring in Mexico* (New York: UN Center on Transnational Corporations, August 1991).

6. Some of these economic activities, categorized in the initial classification chart as "reserved for the Mexican state" (like banking), have subsequently been reconsidered for privatization with a limited percentage of foreign participation.

7. Under Article 23 of the Law, however, foreign ownership of these activities is allowed up to 100 percent through Temporary Investment Trust Funds.

8. Foreign participation in this category is subject to authorization of the National Foreign Investment Commission.

9. Banco de México and Bancomer. It is important to take into consideration that the impressive figure for the first half of 1991 is due in some part to the US$2.7 billion TELMEX stock sale.

10. The impact of this regional agreement in the flow of foreign capital is increased when one takes into account that 66 percent of Mexico's foreign direct investment comes from the United States.

11. Cited in Gabriel Szekely, "Mexico's Challenge: Developing a New International Economic Strategy," in *Changing Networks: Mexico's Telecommunications Options*, eds. Peter F. Cowhey, Jonathan D. Aronson, and Gabriel Szekely (San Diego: Center for U.S.–Mexican Studies, 1989), p. 81.

12. *El Nacional*, October 18, 1990, p. 21.

13. Telecommunications is a sector in which foreigners are allowed to own up to 49 percent of the controlling shares of any Mexican company. See Mexico, Secretariat for Commerce and Industrial Development, *Legal Framework for Direct Foreign Investment in Mexico* (Mexico City, 1990).

14. At the time of TELMEX's privatization (December 1990), AA shares were valued at US$2.03; by mid-March 1991 they were up to US$2.13.

15. *El Nacional*, March 15, 1991, p. 23.

16. Another element that the financial reform of TELMEX brought about was the creation of type L shares. These new L shares are nonvoting shares, and they are valued 2.5 times less than the traditional A TELMEX shares.

17. Each ADS contains twenty L-type shares.

18. *El Nacional*, May 22, 1991, p. 23.

19. Traditionally, market access was linked to the commercial principles of "rights of establishment" and "commercial presence." Today, with the emergence of high-tech telematic networks (telecommunications and informatics), companies are able to provide services from abroad. "Nonestablished" companies do not need to invest in the local economy to provide services in the local market, and the only impediment they have to overcome is acquiring a license to plug into the national public network. See Russel Pipe, *Telecommunications Services: Considerations for Developing Countries in Uruguay Round Negotiations*, report prepared for UNCTAD (Amsterdam, May 1989), and Karl P. Sauvant, *International Transactions in Services: The Politics of Transborder Data Flows* (Boulder, Colo.: Westview Press, 1986).

20. Previously the ownership of the company was distributed, for selected shareholders, as follows: federal government (50.83 percent), Probursa (4.01 percent), Operadora de Bolsa (3.42 percent), Grupo Mexicano de Desarrollo (3.39 percent), Flia. Sáenz (3.32 percent), C.B.I. (3.05 percent), Vector Casa de Bolsa (2.04 percent), Valores Bursatiles (1.74 percent), Inverlat (1.64 percent), Arka (1.53 percent), Abaco (1.32 percent), Estrategia Bursátil (1.20 percent), Prime (1.00 percent), BANAMEX (0.91 percent), Afin (0.85 percent), Inverméxico (0.85 percent), Flia. Bailleres (0.85 percent), Acciones Bursatiles (0.69 percent), Mexival (0.59 percent), Casa Comercial de Bolsa (0.50 percent), Casa de Bolsa Cremi (0.42 percent), Casa de Bolsa México (0.32 percent), others (15.53 percent). See División Académica de Administración y Contaduría, "Cía. Mexicana de Aviación, S.A. de C.V.," mimeo (Mexico City, Instituto Tecnológico Autónomo de México (ITAM), 1990).

21. G.O. (III) Ltd., is an investment company resident in the Cayman Islands.

22. The sale of state-owned enterprises through a large capital increase of the

company is a transfer mechanism not very common in Latin America's privatization programs. Yet, this mode of operation is gaining popularity for certain areas of the economy such as oil, petrochemicals, and mining.

23. The new owners of the reprivatized commercial banks are Multibanco Mercantil de México (Grupo Financiero Probursa/José Madariaga Lomelin), Banpaís (Grupo Mexival/Isidoro Rodríguez), Banca Cremi (Grupo Multiva/Hugo Villa Manzo), Banca Confia (Grupo Abaco/Jorge Lankenau Rocha), Banorie (Grupo Margen/Margain Berlanga), Bancreser (Grupo Roberto Alcántara), and BANAMEX (Grupo Accival/Roberto Hernández and Alfredo Harp Helu). Most of the banks were sold during August 1991, providing the Mexican government with a profit of US$4.3 billion.

24. Still under state control as of October 1991: Bancomer, Banco de Cédulas Hipotecarias, Banco del Atlántico, Comermex, Banca Serfin, Banco Internacional, Banco Sómex, Banorte, Banca Prómex, Banco del Centro, and Banoro.

25. See Mexico, Secretariat of Finance and Public Credit, "El Proceso de Enajenación de Entidades Paraestatales" (Mexico City: Unidad de Desincorporación de Entidades Paraestatales, May 1991).

26. Other companies on line for privatization in the steel sector are Avios de Aceros, S.A.; Carbón y Minerales de Coahuila, S.A.; Cerro del Mercado, S.A.; Cía. Minera El Mamey, S.A.: Cía. Minera La Florida de Múzquiz, S.A.; Consorcio Minero Benito Juárez Pena Colorada, S.A.; Ferroaleaciones de México, S.A.; Hullera Mexicana, S.A.; Internacional de Aceros, S.A.; La Perla Minas de Fierro, S.A.; Minas de California, S.A.; Minera del Norte, S.A.; Minerles de Monclova, S.A.; Refractarios H. W. Flir de México, S.A.; CLEMEX, S.A.; Siderúrgica Nacional, S.A.; and ZINCAMEX 1, S.A.

27. As cited in Uno Mas Uno, March 20, 1991, and Notimex, March 31, 1991.

28. "El Proceso de Enajenación de Entidades Paraestatales," p. 29.

29. In March 1988, Alfonsin's administration signed a letter of intent with Telefónica Internacional, by which the Spanish telecommunications company agreed to purchase a 40 percent stake in ENTEL through an investment program of US$750 million and to assume responsibility for the management of the company.

30. At that time the privatization of state-owned enterprises had to be approved by congress.

31. CAT provides telecommunications services in the provinces of San Juan, Mendoza, Salta, Tucumán, Santiago del Estero, and Entre Ríos.

32. These were names given by the government for sale purposes only.

33. Menem's administration intended in this way to attract U.S. telephone companies, which the administration considered to be the best in the world.

34. Debt papers were bought by the bidders in the secondary market at a highly discounted price (11 cents on the dollar), but taken by the Argentine government at their face value (that is, US$1 each).

35. For a study on the politics of the Argentine telecommunications privatization see Ben A. Petrazzini, "Restructuring Telecommunications Policy in Argentina: An Issue beyond Domestic Concerns," paper presented at the XV Conference of the International Political Association, Buenos Aires, July 1991.

36. The main purchasers of TELECOM probably have diffused their shares as widely as COINTEL has, but this information is not available.

37. This early transfer of shares to the banks in charge of the marketing of ENTEL's shares and the deposit of US$300 million in the state treasury were sparked by regulatory attempts by congress, which threatened the development of the privatization program with a bill that would grant the state control over the 30 percent of shares that constituted the "ENTEL residual."

38. According to studies carried out by the Camara de Informática y Comunicaciones, the Argentine data market has a potential for approximately US$500 million a year. See *El Cronista Comercial*, February 24, 1991, pp. 4–5.

39. The three larger companies are the state-run oil companies of Mexico, Venezuela, and Brazil.

40. YPF sales in 1990 totaled US$5.18 billion, making it Argentina's largest company.

41. The foreign companies participating are Total Austral, S.A. (France) in the area "El Huemel" (US$135 million); Repsol (Spain) in "Vizcacheras" (US$95 million); Santa Fe Energy (U.S.) in "El Tordillo" (US$100 million); and Occidental (U.S.) in "Puesto Hernández" (US$270 million).

42. Telecommunications alone will account for US$300, according to a study developed by the Argentine research institute, Instituto Torcuato Di Tella. See Pablo Gerchunoff and Lilian Castro, "La Racionalidad Macroeconómica de las Privatizaciones: El Caso Argentino," mimeo (Buenos Aires: Instituto Torcuato Di Tella, June 1991).

43. During these years the government received US$2 billion for the privatized companies.

44. Most of these remaining companies were large enterprises accounting for an important share in Chile's economy.

45. For further details on Chile's privatization process, see Pontificia Universidad Católica de Chile, "Aspectos de la Privatización de Empresas Públicas," mimeo (Santiago, Chile, December 1989).

46. The corporation, which is part of a holding with interests in gold, beer, yachts, and finances, is owned by Australian business tycoon Alan Bond.

47. For further details on this issue, see Salomon Brothers, Inc., and International Finance Corporation, "Prospectus on Compañía de Teléfonos de Chile, S.A.," mimeo (New York, 1990).

48. The company is already in Argentina and is interested in Venezuela, Paraguay, and Uruguay and in other telephone companies in Latin America.

49. The first was the privatization of three commercial banks: Banco Occidental de Descuento, Banco Italo Venezolano, and Banco República.

50. Caracas, Maracay, Valencia, Maracaibo, Puerto Ordaz, Barquisimeto, and Barcelona.

51. British and U.S. telecommunications companies control various telephone enterprises in the Caribbean. Cable & Wireless owns telecommunications shares in Jamaica (59 percent of shares), Barbados (65 percent), and St. Kitts and Nevis (80 percent); British Telecom is present in Belize (25 percent); and the U.S.-based GTE

is the sole owner of the telephone company of the Dominican Republic. For a comprehensive study of telecommunications privatization processes in developing countries, see William Ambrose, Paul R. Hennemeyer, and Jean-Paul Chapon, *Privatizing Telecommunications Systems: Business Opportunities in Developing Countries* (Washington, D.C.: World Bank, 1990).

52. Other consortium members are the Overseas Petroleum and Investment Corporation of Taiwan and the North American companies US Maxus Ecuador Inc., Nomeco Ecuador, Murphy, and Canam Offshore. Conoco held 35 percent of the controlling stock in the joint venture.

53. *Petroleum Intelligence Weekly* 30, no. 43 (October 28, 1991), p. 5.

54. These companies were Companhia Siderúrgica de Tubarao; Usinas Siderúrgicas de Minas de Gerais, S.A.; Usinas Mecanicas, S.A.; Maresa, S. A.; Companhia Petroquimica do Nordeste; Petroquisa; Companhia Siderúrgica do Nordeste; Acos Finos Piratini, S.A.; Industria Carboquimica Catarinense, S.A.; Goias Fertilizantes, S.A.; and Mineracao Caraiba Ltda.

55. See Article 13, Law no. 8031/90.

56. Interview with Mexican government official, September 1991.

57. For an extensive analysis of prospective financial flows in Latin America, see Robert Devlin and Martine Guerguil, "América Latina y las Nuevas Corrientes Financieras y Comerciales," *Revista de la CEPAL* 43 (April 1991).

58. Literature presenting the benefits of foreign direct investment in developing countries includes Michael Todaro, *Economic Development in the Third World* (New York: Longman, 1981); Arthur McCormack, *Multinational Investment: Boon and Burden for Developing Countries?* (New York: W. R. Grace & Co., 1980); and Orville L. Freeman, *The Multinational Company: Investment for World Growth* (New York: Praeger, 1981). For a critical approach to the topic, see, for example, Samuel Lichtensztejn, "Inversión Extranjera Directa por Deuda Externa: ¿Freno o Impulso de la Crisis en América Latina?" in *Crisis Financiera y Mecanismos de Contención*, eds. Carlos Tellos Macías and Clemente Ruíz Durán (Mexico City: Fondo de Cultura Económica, 1990); and Theodore H. Moran, *Multinational Corporations: The Political Economy of Foreign Direct Investment* (Lexington, Mass.: Lexington Books, 1985).

59. Devlin and Guerguil, "América Latina y las Nuevas Corrientes," p. 49.

60. Lichtensztejn, "Inversión Extranjera," p. 290.

61. Moran, *Multinational Corporations*, p. 4. Some of these features of foreign direct investment in developing countries can be traced in the privatization of ENTEL (Argentina).

62. Lichtensztejn, "Inversión Extranjera," p. 287.

63. The emergence of this innovative mode of foreign investment has partially shifted the debate on foreign direct investment away from the traditional arguments and focused on debt-related "investments," such as debt-equity swaps.

64. See Joel Bergsman and Wayne Edisis, *Debt-Equity Swaps and FDI in Latin America* (Washington, D.C.: World Bank, 1988), p. 3.

65. Ibid., p. vi.

66. José María Fanelli, Roberto Frenkel, and Guillermo Rozenwurcel, *Growth*

and Structural Reform in Latin America: Where We Stand, Cuadernos CEDES no. 57 (Buenos Aires: CEDES, 1990), p. 65.

67. Some analysts consider this a virtue because it does not add to inflationary pressures in the high-inflation economies of Latin America.

68. See José María Fanelli and Roberto Frenkel, *Un Marco Macroeconómico de Consistencia para el Análisis del Ajuste y el Cambio Estructural en América Latina: Metodología y Hechos Estilizados*, Cuadernos CEDES no. 44 (Buenos Aires: CEDES, 1990).

69. Most Latin American countries require that most profits earned during the first years of the investment be reinvested in the sector.

70. Fanelli, Frenkel, and Rozenwurcel, *Growth and Structural Reform in Latin America*, p. 65.

71. Argentina, for example, has paid, since the 1982 debt crisis, no more than 50 percent of pending interest. During the time that the privatization programs were being implemented, it paid only 15 percent of debt service.

72. Countries that privatize using debt-equity swap operations would take debt paper at face value or nominal value, and not at the price of secondary markets.

73. ECLAC, *Changing Production Patterns with Social Equity* (Santiago, Chile: United Nations, 1990).

74. The lowest for any Latin American country at any time.

75. In the telecommunications sector, for example, approximately forty telephone companies went on sale or were being prepared for sale during the period 1989–1991 alone.

76. The Bank of Mexico requires that 30 percent of credits have to be in cash or government papers like the *Cetes* (*certificados de la Tesorería de la Federación*). As the interest rate difference between loans (35 percent) and deposits (21 percent) was so marked, the new private owners of the banks exceeded the limit of 30 percent. By the end of the month the stock market was affected by a rush of private banks trying to buy *Cetes* papers to reach the 30 percent liquidity, and interest rates skyrocketed to an average of 70 percent. The monetary crisis deepened as a result of further withdrawal of speculative money from the capital market by other financial operators. See Fernando Ortega Pizarro, "El Proyecto Económico de México, en Manos de los Grupos que están Comprando la Banca," *Proceso*, (September 9, 1991), p. 25.

Financial Incentives for Investment in Chile's Privatization

When the Chilean government first opened its banks and public enterprises to privatization, it was greeted with a relative lack of interest on the part of potential buyers and virtually no interest from foreign investors. As a result, incentives had to be offered to entice foreign as well as domestic investment. This chapter presents a review of those incentives, with special attention to implicit subsidies involved in the privatization of US$1.55 billion in public enterprises from 1985 to 1990.

Incentives for Foreign Buyers

Foreign investors wishing to participate in Chile's privatization process face, among others, two important considerations: taxes and earnings repatriation. Incentive structures, first developed by the Chilean government for use in debt capitalization but later used with privatization, have resulted in foreign investment in individual privatized enterprises that has ranged from 20 percent to as much as 100 percent (see table 6.1).

The opinions expressed in this chapter are the responsibility of the author and do not necessarily reflect those of the Corporación de Fomento de la Producción.

TABLE 6.1   Foreign Participation in Privatization in Chile, June 1989

Enterprise	Foreign shareholder	Participation (percentage)	Sale price (million US$)
CAP	Cía. de Inversión Suizandina, S.A.	20.0	
	Inversiones Citicorp Chile, S.A.	2.9	
	Tanner Continental Illionois, S.A.	1.4	
	The Chile Investment Company, S.A.	0.6	
	Total	24.9	109
CHILGENER	Continental International Finance Corp.	20.0	
	Inversiones Financieras SP Chile Ltda.	19.8	
	The Chile Investment Company, S.A.	1.3	
	Total	41.1	
CTC[a]	Bond Corporation Chile, S.A.	48.8	40
ENAEX	Austin Power	67.0	240
IANSA	Continental Finance Corp. II Ltda.	18.4	11
	Tanner Continental Illinois, S.A.	3.1	
	Total	21.5	35
LABCHILE	Continental International Finance Corp.	17.6	
	The Chile Investment Company, S.A.	2.0	
	Total	19.6	14
PILMAIQUEN	I.M. Trust	100.0	n.a.
SOQUIMICH	Capricorn Holding Inc. y Cía. Ltda.	19.8	
	Inversiones ICC Chile Ltda.	2.1	
	Total	21.9	104

a. During 1989 and 1990 there were changes in CTC's ownership structure. Telefónica Internacional Chile, S.A., a subsidiary of Telefónica de España, bought out the share of the Australian group Bond. Shares of CTC were sold on the New York Stock Exchange in the form of American Depositary Receipts (ADRs) and were acquired mainly by the Bank of New York. In December 1990 Telefónica owned 42.83 percent, while the Bank of New York owned 14.71 percent.

NOTE: n.a. = not available.

SOURCES: Dominique Hachette and Rolf Lüders, "Aspects of Privatization: The Case of Chile, 1974–1985," mimeo (Santiago: Pontificia Universidad Católica de Chile, 1988); Bolsa de Comercio de Santiago. *Reseña de Valores* (Santiago, December 1990); and CORFO.

Tax incentives

Tax regime assurances are part of the incentives established for foreign investors. Originally created as a debt-reduction mechanism, these tax incentives have been used for both debt reduction and privatization. Under the incentives, Chile has accumulated debt-equity conversions of US$3.572 billion, or 25 percent of the country's outstanding medium- and long-term external debt. A total of US$143 million has been used for the privatization of seven large companies. This is how, for example, by June 1989, 25 percent of CAP (Compañía de Acero del Pacífico, a steel company) belonged to foreign shareholders, while the Compañía Telefónica de España held 43 percent of CTC (Compañía de Teléfonos de Chile) in December 1990 (see table 6.1).

Current regulations and earnings repatriation

Under Chapters XVIII and XIX of the Foreign Exchange Regulations, the central bank regulates the foreign acquisition of promissory notes of the Chilean foreign debt. In order to buy shares of a Chilean firm, foreigners must first purchase promissory notes, which are sold at a discount (around 11 percent). The promissory notes are then brought into the country through the banking system and converted into local currency at their face value, to be used to buy the domestic shares. Foreign investors who use this method must file a request with the central bank providing all pertinent information regarding the promissory notes and the investment involved. After approval, the central bank guarantees access to the official exchange market in order to transfer abroad the capital invested and profits earned from the investment, subject to the following conditions:

- Capital may not be repatriated until ten years after the investment has entered the country.

- Foreign exchange used to repatriate the capital may only be obtained with the proceeds of a total or partial sale of shares.

- Profits earned during the first four years may not be remitted abroad until the fifth year, with an annual ceiling of 25 percent of accumulated earnings. Profits earned from the fifth year on are not subject to these restrictions.

Incentives for Domestic Buyers

Incentives for local buyers were aimed at three clearly identifiable groups: employees of the public enterprises to be privatized, purchasers on the stock exchange, and pension fund administrators. These incentives included the following:

- If companies had never gone public before, stock subscriptions were priced lower than the economic value, which was estimated on the basis of expected profits.

- Credit at below-market rates was provided by the central bank and CORFO (Corporación de Fomento de la Producción), a government-owned development bank and holding company.

- Special tax credits were afforded to shareholders.

- Employees received advance payment of compensation for their years of service, a key component of their pensions. The financial provisions maintained by the privatizing enterprises themselves for these liabilities could be similarly used. Advance payments carry the restriction, however, that at least 80 percent of the payment must be used for the acquisition of shares.

- Through collective bargaining, it could be stipulated that employee bonuses be paid in shares instead of money.

- Financial contributions, which are an exchange of an investment required by the users of a public service for a share in the capital of the enterprise, were reimbursable.

- Decrease of capital was used only for CAP, and consisted of reducing the share capital so that the private participation rate climbed from 13 percent to 49 percent, while CORFO's participation was reduced from 87 percent to 51 percent.

- Specific projects were financed by auction of newly issued share packages, which is being touted by the present government as an alternative method of privatization, tied to new investment.

Involving workers in the process leads to a wider diffusion of the holdings, which has been one of the primary objectives of the Chilean privatization program. Several barriers have had to be overcome, however. Workers often did not have the necessary resources to acquire shares in their enterprises. Thus, incentives and tax exemptions were needed in addition to an attractive price. To this end, incentives such as the advance payments, payment of bonuses in shares, and, in particular, special credit conditions were implemented. This special credit has been granted principally by CORFO or by the enterprise itself.

In addition to the incentives already mentioned, workers who hold shares in the company are allowed to participate in the direction of the enterprise. Moreover, they are given a measure of security if they hold their shares until retirement, because the enterprise pledges to reimburse workers the full value of their initial purchase if there is any capital loss.

A special case involves the reprivatization of the banks that were placed under government control during the economic crisis of 1982. During that time, as a result of a recession and loan defaults by the private sector, many financial institutions could not honor their commitments. Several enterprises went bankrupt or suffered large losses. This led the state to intervene by taking control of the banks.

In 1985, once the crisis had been completely overcome, Law 18,401 was adopted to reprivatize these institutions and disseminate their property. This became known as "popular capitalism." Under the law, CORFO was given the authority to extend credits to contributors that were current in their obligations. These credits carried extremely beneficial provisions. In the case of Banco de Chile and Banco de Santiago, terms were a 5 percent cash down payment, with the balance due over fifteen years and without any real interest (that is, at an interest rate just equal to the rate of inflation). This was in addition to a 30 percent discount on installments paid on time.

Furthermore, there were strong tax incentives for investing in these two banks. First, dividend payments valued at less than 30 percent of each bank's annual profits were not subject to income taxes. Second, 20 percent of the investment in the shares of the banks could be deducted from the income tax base. This meant a considerable subsidy to the private sector. In the following section we will see in more detail the extent of this and other implicit subsidies.

Implicit Subsidies in Privatization

The government provides three main types of implicit subsidies. Each type is defined below, and methods of calculation are explained. (Examples of the calculation of each type of subsidy are provided in tables A6.1–A6.4 in the appendix following this chapter.) The subsidies described are implicit subsidies, not direct cash rewards. Also, all subsidies are *ex ante*, meaning they are calculated from the best information available at the time of the investment. Thus, the calculation of the economic subsidy is based on future dividends from expected profits and the cost of capital at the time each package of shares is sold. This also applies to the rates and expected taxes used in the calculation of the financial and fiscal subsidies.

An economic subsidy is the present value of the difference between the enterprise's economic value and the actual price of the sale. At least two methods exist to measure economic value. One is market price, which is assumed to reflect the value of the enterprise as it is perceived by investors.

This method is not feasible, however, in cases where shares have never been sold before. In the calculations here, market price was used only for the years 1988 and 1989 and only for those enterprises that had a sufficient number of existing shares.

A second method of determining economic value is to calculate the present value of the estimated future flow of the stock's dividends. To arrive at this, we first calculate the estimated dividends and then apply the relevant interest rate for the period.[1] A second criterion used was the market perception of the book value for the corresponding year, calculated on the basis of the proportion between the stock exchange value and the average book value for the enterprises traded on the stock exchange for each year.

A financial subsidy is the present value of the flow of net income arising from credit granted with special provisions, such as at interest rates lower than the market rates, payment discounts for installments paid on time, or grace periods. In general, this credit was extended by CORFO or by the enterprise itself. A special case is that of the banks taken over by the government, as discussed above.

A fiscal subsidy is the present value of income tax credits originating in the acquisition of shares of the reprivatized banks (Banco de Chile and Banco de Santiago). The size of the subsidy depends on the contributor's tax bracket, since that determines the marginal rate of taxes. This benefit is to be in place for eight years.

It is important to note that government capital losses, although linked to, are not necessarily equivalent to private gains, since cash flows or discount rates may differ. Moreover, eventual increases in future tax receipts may mitigate the negative effect that these subsidies could generate.

Estimation of Implicit Subsidies

Using the previous definitions, the different types of subsidies for enterprises privatized between 1985 and 1989 can be calculated. Tables 6.2 and 6.3 summarize the results of the privatization process in Chile during this period. The principal aim of the tables is to illustrate the implicit costs that the state incurred to transfer the enterprises into private hands.

Table 6.2 shows the participation of CORFO in the privatized enterprises and the value of the economic subsidy, calculated as explained above. The table also shows the form in which the enterprises were sold, the percentage sold, the sum at which they were sold, and how much credit was granted by CORFO. Table 6.3 presents the subsidies for nonfinancial enterprises. The total economic subsidy was 8.1 percent of the

TABLE 6.2 State Participation in and Sales of State-owned Enterprises, 1985–1989

Firm	Economic value (thousand US$)	CORFO participation (at beginning of privatization)		Economic value of CORFO sales		Effective price (Thousand US$)	CORFO credit	
		Percentage	Thousand US$	Percentage[a]	Thousand US$		Percentage of sale[b]	Thousand US$
CAP[c]	115,176	94.6	108,957	94.6	108,957	70,801		
CHILGENER[c]	71,445	99.4	71,017	99.4	71,017	57,836		
CHILMETRO[c]	125,143	99.4	124,392	99.4	124,392	86,449		
CHILQUINTA[c]	27,563	99.4	27,398	99.4	27,398	20,183		
CTC[c]	283,875	83.6	237,320	83.5	237,036	292,770	3.0	8,809
ECOM[d]	1,846	100.0	1,846	100.0	1,846	2,074	83.3	1,728
EDELMAG[d]	9,158	87.6	8,022	87.6	8,022	3,234	84.9	2,747
ELECDA[d]	10,070	86.1	8,671	86.1	8,671	3,206	96.7	3,099
ELIQSA[d]	5,192	86.1	4,471	86.1	4,471	3,351	53.3	1,787
EMELARI[d]	4,739	86.1	4,080	86.1	4,080	3,140	55.5	1,744
ENAEX[d]	6,314	95.4	6,024	95.4	6,024	7,438	57.4	4,267
ENDESA[c]	478,991	99.0	474,201	98.0	469,411	498,492	28.2	140,424
ENTEL[c]	178,700	99.9	178,521	99.6	177,985	144,537		
IANSA[c]	46,986	99.7	46,845	99.7	46,845	37,352		
LABCHILE[c]	14,168	97.1	13,757	97.1	13,757	14,632		
PEHUENCHE[d]	105,016	70.0	73,511	70.0	73,511	51,627		
SOQUIMICH[c]	184,092	93.0	171,206	93.0	171,206	131,923		
Total	1,668,474	93.5	1,560,200	93.2	1,554,590	1,429,043	11.5	164,605

a. Percentage of the economic value of the enterprise.
b. Percentage of the total of the sale.
c. The estimated value for 1985 is calculated based on the market perception as a percentage of the book value; for the years 1986 and 1987 data from Hachette and Lüders, "Aspects of Privatization," were used; for the years 1988 and 1989 market price criteria were used.
d. Economic value is assumed to be the market perception as a percentage of book value in each year according to the average of ratios actually observed in the stock exchange.

NOTE: Blank indicates zero.

SOURCES: CORFO and Dominique Hachette and Rolf Lüders, "Aspects of Privatization: The Case of Chile, 1974–1985," mimeo (Santiago: Pontificia Universidad Católica de Chile, 1988).

103

TABLE 6.3   Implicit Subsidies in Sales of State-owned Enterprises

| Enterprise | Economic subsidy | | Financial subsidy | | Total |
	Thousand US$[a]	Percentage[b]	Thousand US$	Percentage[c]	(thousand US$)
CAP[d]	38,156	35.0			38,156
CHILGENER[d]	13,181	18.6			13,181
CHILMETRO[d]	37,943	30.5			37,943
CHILQUINTA[d]	7,215	26.3			7,215
CTC[d]	−55,734	−23.5	1,365	15.5	−54,369
ECOM[e]	−228	−12.3	158	9.2	−70
EDELMAG[e]	4,788	59.7	464	17.0	5,252
ELECDA[e]	5,465	63.0	455	14.7	5,920
ELIQSA[e]	1,120	25.1	265	14.9	1,385
EMELARI[e]	940	23.0	251	14.4	1,191
ENAEX[e]	−1,415	−23.5	43	1.0	−1,372
ENDESA[d]	−29,081	−6.2	27,879	19.4	−1,202
ENTEL[d]	33,448	18.8			33,448
IANSA[d]	9,492	20.3			9,492
LABCHILE[d]	−874	−6.4			−874
PEHUENCHE[e]	21,884	29.8			21,884
SOQUIMICH[d]	39,283	22.9			39,283
Total	125,584	8.1	30,880	18.8	156,464

a. Obtained by subtracting the economic value from the cash value of the sale.
b. Percentage of the economic value of the total sale.
c. Percentage of the total debt.
d. The estimated value for 1985 is calculated based on the market perception as percentage of book value; data for 1986 and 1987 were obtained from Hachette and Lüders, "Aspects of Privatization"; for the years 1988 and 1989 market price criteria were used.
e. Economic value is assumed to be the market perception as a percentage of book value in each year according to the average of cash ratios observed on the stock exchange.
NOTE: Blank indicates zero. Figures may not add because of rounding.
SOURCES: CORFO and Dominique Hachette and Rolf Lüders, "Aspects of Privatization: The Case of Chile, 1974–1985," mimeo (Santiago: Pontificia Universidad Católica de Chile, 1988).

value of the sales, and the financial subsidy was 18.8 percent of the total credit. This is equivalent to a total subsidy for the sale of nonfinancial enterprises of US$156 million, or 10.1 percent of the economic value of the sales.

Banks were reprivatized under special conditions and therefore were analyzed separately. Table 6.4 presents general information on the process for five banks. Table 6.5 shows the financial and fiscal subsidies involved in the reprivatization. The subsidy was 80.7 percent of the total of the sales. The total subsidy, for financial and nonfinancial enterprises, is 22.6 percent of the sales.

Final Comments

As a result of Chile's privatization program, fewer productive assets currently remain in state hands, and former state companies are now fairly well dispersed. Thus, the present government's efforts now focus on boosting net private investment, both foreign and domestic, and on new projects, rather than on selling old shares.

The main areas of investment being offered by the state are in utilities such as water, sewage treatment, and electric power, and in infrastructure work for ports and highways. Private participation in the utilities is open in the share capital of state-owned enterprises, while in the case of infrastructure, the establishment of concession contracts to individual investors is also being sought.

The financing of the privatizations during the authoritarian regime that governed Chile until 1990 was sometimes criticized as contradicting the interests of the state by transferring hidden subsidies to the private sector. Also questioned was the fact that managers appointed by the old government to head the state enterprises subsequently became owners of large portions of the companies privatized under their own management. Although this last point has not been addressed here, it could be as important as the implicit subsidies when it comes to the legitimization of the privatization process. Public opinion surveys reveal that 55 percent oppose the simple sale of old shares in public enterprises, but strong support exists for the efficient direction of and private participation in the state enterprises.

The Chilean case shows a high degree—80 percent—of subsidized financing in the case of the banks. Nonfinancial enterprises, which were in a better situation than the financial enterprises when they were put on sale, required subsidies of only 10 percent. The latter amount does not seem unduly large if it is assumed that eventual efficiency gains will generate larger future tax revenues for the state. Whether this occurs or not is the responsibility not only of the new enterprises but also of the

TABLE 6.4   Conditions for Reprivatization of Banks

Bank	Number of shares (millions)	Percentage privatized	Number of operations	Value of shares sold on credit		Term (years)	Interest rate (percentage)
				Million US$	Percentage[a]		
BHIF[b]	1,238	99.0	296	12	100.0	15	5.0
Chile[c]	11,000	90.5	28,000	177	95.0	15	0.0
Concepcion	228	95.1	1	29	100.0	20	0.0
Internacional	238	95.0	112	4	100.0	15	0.0
Santiago[c]	11,400	97.4	18,000	120	95.0	15	0.0
Total	24,104		46,409	342			

a. Percentage of the total sale.
b. 10 percent discount for on-time installment payment.
c. 30 percent discount for on-time installment payment.
SOURCE: CORFO.

TABLE 6.5   Financial and Fiscal Subsidies in the Sale of Banks

| Bank | Financial subsidy | | Fiscal subsidy | | Total |
	Thousand US$	Percentage[a]	Thousand US$	Percentage[b]	(thousand US$)
BHIF	2,986	24.3			2,986
Chile	101,290	60.3	50,536	28.6	151,826
Concepcion	16,259	57.8			16,259
Internacional	1,352	41.8			1,352
Santiago	68,860	60.3	34,356	28.6	103,216
Total	190,747	50.5	84,892	28.6	275,639

a. Percentage of the total debt.
b. Percentage of the investment of cash value of the sale.
NOTE: Blank indicates zero.
SOURCE: CORFO.

government, which is charged with the general administration of the economy.

The Chilean privatization experience should be judged as successful, at least as regards nonfinancial enterprises. This gives rise to a second step of private participation: the financing of new projects. In this undertaking, privatization combined with investment will be the biggest priority.

Note

1. Dominique Hachette and Rolf Lüders, "Aspects of Privatization: The Case of Chile, 1974–1985," mimeo (Santiago: Pontificia Universidad Católica de Chile, 1988).

Appendix

TABLE A6.1 Calculation of Economic Subsidies, Nonfinancial Enterprises, 1985–1989 (thousand UF[a] unless otherwise indicated)

Sale of CTC

	1985[b]	1986/87[c]	1988[d]	1989[d]	Total	Total (thousand US$)
Shares sold (1,000)	1,814.4	56,792.5	248,545.6	71,278.2	378,430.7	
Percentage sold	0.5	14.1	53.5	15.4	83.5	
Estimated price	24.7	2,032.6	8,533.3	2,411.8	13,002.5	237,036.0
Effective price	19.9	2,145.1	10,648.3	3,246.5	16,059.8	292,769.7
Economic subsidy	4.9	−112.5	−2,114.9	−834.6	−3,057.3	−55,733.7

Sale of ENTEL

	1985[b]	1986/87[c]	1988[d]	1989[d]	Total	Total (thousand US$)
Shares sold (1,000)	1,111.5	30,278.8	29,202.5	33,733.7	94,326.5	
Percentage sold	0.2	32.7	30.3	36.4	99.6	
Estimated price	2.9	2,644.9	2,872.6	4,242.9	9,763.3	177,984.9
Effective price	5.6	1,528.7	2,872.9	3,521.4	7,928.5	292,769.7
Economic subsidy	−2.7	1,116.2	−0.3	721.5	1,834.8	33,447.5

Sale of ENDESA

	1985[b]	1986/87[c]	1988[d]	1989[d]	Total	Total (thousand US$)
Shares sold (1,000)	0	1,808,612.0	5,494,750.0	521,323.8	7,824,686	
Percentage sold	0	22.0	69.4	6.6	98	
Estimated price		6,150.7	17,704.4	1,894.3	25,749.4	469,410.8
Effective price		6,855.4	18,375.8	2,113.4	27,344.6	498,492.0
Economic subsidy		−704.8	−671.4	−219.0	−1,595.2	−29,081.1

(continued)

Table A6.1 (continued)

	1985[b]	1986/87[c]	1988[d]	1989[d]	Total	Total (thousand US$)
Sale of CAP						
Shares sold (1,000)	28,923.8	132,104.5	0	0	161,028.3	
Percentage sold	7.0	87.6	0	0	94.6	
Estimated price	1,045.2	4,931.8			5,976.8	108,956.7
Effective price	363.7	3,520.1			3,883.8	70,800.9
Economic subsidy	681.5	1,411.7			2,093.0	38,155.9
Sale of SOQUIMICH						
Shares sold (1,000)	0	92,567.1	22,210.9	0	114,778.0	
Percentage sold	0	75.0	18.0	0	93.0	
Estimated price		7,491.3	1,900.2		9,391.4	171,205.7
Effective price		5,156.7	2,079.9		7,236.6	131,923.0
Economic subsidy		2,334.5	−179.7		2,154.8	39,282.7
Sale of CHILGENER						
Shares sold (1,000)	669.0	11,843.7	2,919.7	0	15,432.3	
Percentage sold	4.3	76.3	18.8	0	99.4	
Estimated price	177.5	3,218.5	499.6		3,895.6	71,016.5
Effective price	103.8	2,441.0	627.8		3,172.6	57,835.8
Economic subsidy	73.7	777.5	−128.2		723.0	13,180.7

a. UF is the Chilean indexation unit and is equivalent to a one-month lagged CPI. It is worth approximately US$21.
b. Estimated price according to "market perception," namely a percentage of book value in each year according to the average of cash ratios in the stock exchange (the exchange book relation for June 1985 is 32%).
c. Estimation by Dominique Hachette and Rolf Lüders, "Aspects of Privatization: The Case of Chile, 1974–1985," mimeo (Santiago: Pontificia Universidad Católica de Chile, 1988).
d. Estimated price according to market value.
Note: Figures may not add because of rounding.
Source: Author's calculations.

Package	Rate[a] (%)	Term (years)	Sale value (thousand US$)	Annual flow (thousand US$)	Discounted flow (thousand US$)
A	2.0	6	2,046	365	1,618
B	3.0	5	4,103	896	3,446
C	4.5	4	2,661	742	2,380
Total			8,809		7,444

TABLE A6.2   Calculation of Financial Subsidies, Nonfinancial Enterprise (CTC sold to armed forces), 1989

NOTE: Figures may not add because of rounding.
Subsidy value
    Debt amount   US$8,809,000
    Present value of debt US$7,444,000
    Subsidy   US$1,365,000
    Percentage   15.50
a. Average annual interest rate: 9.43%
SOURCE: Author's calculations.

TABLE A6.3   Calculation of Financial Subsidies, Financial Enterprise (Banco de Santiago)

Year	Flows, including 30% discount (thousand US$)	Discount factor	Discounted flows (thousand US$)
1	5,325	1.0812	4,925
2	5,325	1.1690	4,555
3	5,325	1.2639	4,213
4	5,325	1.3665	3,897
5	5,325	1.4775	3,604
6	5,325	1.5975	3,333
7	5,325	1.7272	3,083
8	5,325	1.8674	2,851
9	5,325	2.0191	2,637
10	5,325	2.1830	2,439
11	5,325	2.3603	2,256
12	5,325	2.5520	2,087
13	5,325	2.7592	1,930
14	5,325	2.9832	1,785
15	5,325	3.2255	1,651
Total			45,247

NOTE: Sale price: US$120,113,000
    Cash: 5% (US$6,006,000)
    Conditions: credit, 0.00% interest, 15 years, equal annuities, 30% discount for on-time payments
    Buyers: individuals
    Average annual interest rate, 1985–1987: 8.12%
Subsidy value
    Debt amount   US$114,107,000
    Present value of debt US$45,247,000
    Subsidy   US$68,860,000
    Percentage   60.3
SOURCE: Author's calculations.

TABLE A6.4   Calculation of Tax Subsidies, Financial Enterprise
              (Banco de Santiago)

Year	Discount on base (20% of investment, in thousand US$)	Flow of tax savings (25%,[a] in thousand US$)	Factor discount	Discounted flow (thousand US$)
1	24,023	6,006	1.08	5,555
2	24,023	6,006	1.17	5,137
3	24,023	6,006	1.26	4,752
4	24,023	6,006	1.37	4,395
5	24,023	6,006	1.48	4,065
6	24,023	6,006	1.60	3,759
7	24,023	6,006	1.73	3,477
8	24,023	6,006	1.87	3,216
Total				34,356

NOTE: Investment: US$120,113,000
Tax base discount: 20%
Marginal tax rate: 25%
Flow of savings from taxes: US$6,006,000
Discount rate (average 1985–1987): 8.12%
Present value of savings: US$34,356,000
Fiscal subsidy: US$34,356,000
Percentage: 28.60

a. Marginal tax rate of 25%, corresponding to incomes in the range of US$7,365,000 to US$10,311,000 annually.

SOURCE: Author's calculations.

PART TWO

OPENING LATIN AMERICA'S ECONOMIC SECTORS TO FOREIGN PRIVATE INVESTMENT

Privatization as an Objective: Telecommunications and Regulatory Reform

Regulatory structures play an important but often overlooked role in telecommunications privatizations. A sound regulatory structure is critical to the promotion of long-term sector growth, economic expansion, and the realization of certain societal and political objectives in the construction and operation of the telecommunications network. Regulatory structures implemented primarily to serve an initial privatization transaction, if not properly established, may entrench inefficient industry relationships, thus substantially limiting opportunities for future telecommunications growth and thwarting or delaying the achievement of national goals. If carefully designed, however, regulatory structures can foster development and ensure achievement of privatization objectives for the long term.

The challenge for decision makers is to identify the specific needs of a particular country and to adapt solutions and approaches to the country's individual circumstances. In this chapter we offer some basic guidelines for meeting this challenge. Our theme is that in most markets the introduction of competition and the reliance on marketplace forces will benefit both service providers and users. Regulatory structures should be aimed to achieve this result. Particularly in the developing world, however, careful consideration must be given to ensuring the expansion of basic services. Competition must therefore be introduced judiciously. This requires a careful balancing of objectives and phased implementation of policies by a strong regulator guided by well-articulated, long-term objectives.

The Objective of Privatization

Privatization is both a process and an ultimate objective. As a process, it involves complex risk analyses and intricate transactional activities. As an objective, privatization means a fundamental change in the incentives and goals that govern management.

Under state ownership, management incentives and objectives are defined by social policy and often are implemented by inefficient bureaucracies. In today's global market, it is not enough for privatization to effect a transition from public, or state, ownership to private ownership. Public monopolies and private monopolies both tend to be bureaucratic and inefficient. The real significance of privatization is to obtain for the public and for the market as a whole the full range of benefits of the incentives that drive competitive private enterprise. These include innovation, investment, efficiency, and responsiveness to market needs.

By the sheer force of the unrelenting march of technological development and the irrepressible demands of increasingly multinational business users, administrations will be required to admit more participants and to break down monopolies. Telecommunications markets all over the world are expanding by leaps and bounds and are becoming less homogeneous and more varied and complex. Telecommunications serve many needs in many ways. In very few of these ways are telecommunications arguably still a "natural monopoly." The full benefit of all of the varied facets of telecommunications cannot be achieved through monopoly. Rather, it must be achieved through the accommodation and even promotion of multiple voices.

The proper focus of privatization therefore is not merely on the single transaction that retires debt or unburdens the government from an expensive enterprise. Instead, the focus must be on the establishment of structures intended to encourage and foster the most positive traits of private enterprise and market forces.

The Function of Telecommunications and the Importance of Infrastructure

Privatization has special significance in the telecommunications sector. This is because the value of telecommunications transcends the value of copper wire, microwave links, switches, and earth stations. It even transcends the value of the exchange of messages, whether by voice, facsimile, data, video, telex, or other means. The value of telecommunications is its ability to form the glue of society and the foundation of domestic and international commerce. Telecommunications services are fast becoming the very foundation, not only of commercial transactions and economic growth, but also of the delivery of educational programs, health services, news and information, arts and culture, and emergency aid. Telecommunications services not only improve the quality of life, but also can help to save lives. In this context advanced telecommunications in the modern multinational environment are becoming less of a luxury and more of a necessity.

The value of telecommunications services is inextricably linked to the geographic breadth, technological capabilities, and flexibility of the network over which those services are provided. The inherent value of telecommunications is the facilitation of communication among an increasing universe of users and through an increasing variety of means. This extension of the network defines its strength as an infrastructure. Infrastructure thus refers to the value of the network as a resource, not only for the provision of particular services, but for the expansion of value to each user of the extended reach of a single interconnected network. The value of the network to every participant increases exponentially with the addition of other users and the access to ever more sophisticated services. It should be the highest and ultimate objective of any administration engaging in privatization to foster the growth and development of this value in the telecommunications network infrastructure for all citizens. The challenge is to do so in a way that effectively balances the strength of a centrally planned and operated telecommunications system with the benefits that reliance on market forces can provide.

What balance must be struck? It is one between the promotion of private commercial aspects of competitive markets and the achievement of reasonable social goals. On the side of commercialization, decision makers should create attractive financial incentives for efficient operation, technical innovation, and plant modernization as well as establish reasonable and rational price structures, standards for service flexibility, and ease of technical interconnection. On the side of meeting social goals, decision makers must promote incentives for extension of affordable service and targeting of necessary subsidies. They must also avoid diversion of lucrative traffic from the public switched network for uneconomic reasons. Thus, at the same time that decision makers must find a solution that achieves a successful privatization and that promotes efficiency and private investment profitability, they must also erect a regulatory structure that ensures meeting social goals. The ideal is to foster a network that can serve the most sophisticated multinational business user with interactive and integrated digital services while also providing the most remote rural low-income user with "lifeline" access to basic telephone services. Only regulatory frameworks that are properly designed and implemented from the beginning can transform this ideal into reality.

The Challenge of Latin America

In Latin America the telecommunications infrastructure must not only be protected and preserved, but in many places must still be built. A pervasive problem in Latin America is that both residential and business subscribers suffer inadequate service. In contrast to developed countries such as the United States, which has well over 90 percent penetration, provision of basic services in most Latin American countries is closer to 10 percent. Residential users suffer long waits for installation of a telephone, and once they get a telephone, service is often unreliable. For example, in Argentina prior to the recent sale of ENTEL, the installation backlog was in excess of four years, the average wait for repair was 14.5 days, and the efficiency of local calls was only 47 percent.

Other Latin American countries have similar problems. Businesses usually suffer for lack of reliable international interconnections and the inability to reduce expenses by owning terminal equipment located on their own premises. Perhaps most critically, business services lack digital switching and processing capabilities needed for access to valuable information services and databases worldwide. This inefficiency then becomes distributed through the products and services that underlie the nation's economy.

Service to rural areas remains an important social goal. Yet these areas are usually more costly to reach and to serve as a result of a combination of factors, including unavailability of economic technology, such as high-powered domestic satellites, low traffic volumes, and high maintenance expenses. Telecommunications networks built largely on the public ownership model (governed by social goals), rather than a truly private system model (governed by market responsiveness), tend to waste valuable resources. Unfocused and poorly targeted subsidy mechanisms unfairly burden existing system subscribers and result in underutilization of a network whose costs are largely fixed, whether used or not. Badly targeted subsidies mean that less assistance reaches those areas most in need.

The United States learned this lesson well. It has now succeeded in making a difficult but important transition from the old integrated Bell System infused with nontargeted subsidies to an industry structure and pricing system that channels support directly to those mostly in need. This change has unburdened businesses and large users so the efficiencies of well-managed telecommunications networks can be filtered through the entire economy.

The challenge of Latin America is to move from the public to the private model, while at the same time addressing these fundamental service requirements. The developed countries have had the advantage of building on substantial existing networks in their transition to competitive, privatized markets. Developing countries find themselves trying to leapfrog into a privatized structure that accommodates both the competition needed to meet business user demands and the extension of basic service to residential and rural subscribers. Only a carefully designed, flexible legal and regulatory framework, coupled with a fair and open regulatory process, can realize these goals.

The Focus of Regulatory Reform and the Myth of Deregulation

Historically the focus of regulation has been to ensure that a "natural" monopoly service, which affects the public interest, is actually provided in a way that serves established social goals. As services, networks, and technologies have become more advanced and complex, and as certain markets have become increasingly competitive, the role of regulation has changed. In the modern era the role of the regulator is not just to ensure that a monopoly acts in the public interest, but also to facilitate and foster growth, technical innovation, efficiency, and user responsiveness. Thus, the focus of regulation has shifted from a patronizing overview of company operations toward a more incisive policing of boundaries between the shrinking realm of natural monopoly and the expanding universe of competitive services.

The great challenge to regulators is to find the proper balance between services that should keep some vestige of monopoly on the one hand and the development of competition on the other. This requires the protection of the public infrastructure from uneconomic bypass through the implementation of rational rate structures and enforcement of nondiscriminatory technical interconnection. It also requires that the regulator promote entry into the marketplace by minimizing regulation where it is counterproductive and by facilitating the introduction of new technologies and services through the maintenance of expedient processing procedures and coordinated frequency allocation.

It is a myth of deregulation that liberalization of telecommunications markets and the opening of opportunities for competitive entry will decrease requirements for regulatory oversight, at least in the short and medium term. Especially in markets where social objectives must be defined and achieved in a mixed industry structure containing some elements of monopoly and some of competition, the task of the regulator is extremely difficult, yet of utmost importance. The regulator must pay scrupulous attention to transactions between these monopoly and competitive elements. Carrying out this task requires several things:

- It requires extraordinary diligence and creativity in the establishment of cost allocation standards, accounting requirements, and other techniques for detecting and policing subsidies and all forms of anticompetitive pricing activities by the monopoly provider.

- It also requires the capacity to analyze and process competing requests for frequency allocation and to achieve and enforce technical standards that are sufficient to ensure nondiscriminatory interconnection but that do not inefficiently burden the industry. The regulator must establish particular standards to detect and penalize all forms of anticompetitive behavior, including abuse of ownership and operation of local "bottleneck" facilities and the improper use of customer proprietary information.

- It requires the capacity to classify and reclassify services in flexible response to market developments and technical change.

- It requires the ability to establish rational and targeted subsidies for high-cost subscribers, particularly for systems in rural areas.

- Above all, it requires the endowment of a regulatory entity with enough resources to undertake the formidable task of actually regulating a nationwide telecommunications system. Care must be taken not to saddle the regulatory entity with tasks that it cannot meet, lest it be rendered ineffective.

Key Elements of an Effective Regulatory Structure

Under the pressured circumstances of privatization, goals associated with telecommunications regulatory reform can easily become confused. Privatization is not synonymous with regulatory reform. The goals associated with achieving a short-term maximization of value in the sale of assets are not the same as achieving maximization of the value of infrastructure over the long term. In many cases it would be far preferable to have regulatory reform initiated long before the privatization process. This would permit the identification of goals and the establishment of an industry structure that reflects long-term telecommunications sector objectives.

Many countries that recently have attempted to capitalize on the momentum of privatization initiatives have not been able to allow themselves the luxury of early regulatory reform. Other countries that view privatization as a future prospect would do well to begin the process of evaluating their objectives for industry structure and the options for a regulatory framework now. If the prospect of having to decide everything at once is simply unavoidable, policy makers must identify the specific goals and objectives for the telecommunications sector at the outset of the process. Failure to take this step could endanger the growth of the infrastructure. It could also be a substantial deterrent to foreign investors or to potential purchasers. Well-formulated policy objectives will provide clarity and guidance in establishing the regulatory structure.

Establishment of clear goals

The first step toward the establishment of reasonable goals is to take a comprehensive inventory of the status of the network and the needs of the country. Quantitative aspects such as numbers of lines served, waiting time for installation, and percentage of call completion are important statistics. Qualitative factors are equally important. The existing structure of the industry, including common ownership of local, long-distance, and/ or international operations, is an important determinant of the future flexibility and growth of the network structure. The existing network structure may dictate the ease with which additional independent parties may be permitted or encouraged to enter specific markets such as rural services and even the more competitive and profitable international services. The status and inventory of network and transmission equipment will indicate where the requirements for investment are most critical. Other qualitative factors, including geography, demography, topography, and climate will affect objectives for extension of lines and development of rural services. Markets for private networks and value-added services should also be assessed. Special issues such as the concerns of labor unions and historical aspects of handling questions concerning frequency allocation and rate structure will affect expectations for improved efficiency in the near term. Finally, the jurisdiction and participation of state or other local authorities will also affect the development of an overall sector plan.

Following the completion of an inventory, short-term and long-term goals should be separately identified. Short-term goals are likely to include the promotion of capital investment and the extension of lines. Such goals may be developed in qualitative as well as in quantitative terms. For example, an objective for extension of service may include the addition of a certain number of lines per year, but the service required to be provided may be defined as basic access with a limited number of calls. For rural areas limited access to basic services may be appropriate, with the focus on long-distance capabilities. Other short-term goals include network improvements required for business services to alleviate long-distance and international bottlenecks.

In the major Latin American privatizations, various goals have been set. For example, in Argentina the government established very particular service obligations for the new telephone enterprises, TELECOM and Telefónica. The new companies must achieve an installation time of fifteen days, a repair time of one day, 80 percent efficiency on repair and information calls, and 98 percent efficiency on local and long-distance calls. The licensees are obligated to monitor the attainment of service goals and to report to the regulatory body on an annual basis.

Similarly, in Mexico, with a penetration rate of approximately 10 percent and only 5 percent digital switching equipment, the government established both quantitative and qualitative service improvements obligations for the privatized TELMEX. TELMEX must extend fiber optic networks, digitalize microwave systems, and install satellite communications stations. The company is required to average 12 percent annual growth over the period 1991 to 1995, and 2.7 million lines must be added to the system. TELMEX must reduce ordering time from 1.5 years to six months by 1994 and to one month by the year 2000. TELMEX must also provide the smallest towns with at least a telephone booth and larger towns with modernized exchange facilities.

Long-term goals include the establishment of rational economic support for "universal service," however defined, and the promotion of efficiency, innovation, and domestic and international interconnectivity. These long-term goals are best served by the introduction of competition. In order to successfully introduce competition, however, the regulatory framework will have to provide for reorganization and rationalization of subsidy systems, balanced rate structures that reflect cost characteristics and technical standards, and a network architecture that permits fair interconnection.

Creation of a strong regulatory agency

The ultimate objective in establishing an effective regulatory entity is to give it sufficient powers for effective, quick decision making while also requiring that regulatory intervention in market relationships be minimized to the greatest extent possible. This balancing begins with goals that are clearly set out in the enabling legal documents, whether they are presidential decrees, statutes, or ministry regulations.

A detailed treatment of the structural and procedural attributes of regulatory entities is well beyond the scope of this chapter. Certain key features can be identified, however. First, the goals that are established to guide the entity should include availability of affordable basic service to all citizens, fair and equitable technical and market circumstances to encourage competitive entry (without penalizing efficiency), and technical innovation.

Second, the regulatory entity should function as independently as the country's legal framework will allow. Independence of decision making leads to policies that best serve the telecommunications sector rather than unwise or shortsighted political concerns. Part of the independence of the regulatory agency also derives from the mechanisms established to ensure continued and adequate funding. The regulatory entity should have its own budget and ideally should be funded directly both through government appropriations and through receipts from various fees charged to licensees. It also may be most efficient to combine regulation of telecommunications with certain aspects of regulation of mass media, particularly with respect to the allocation of radio frequency spectrum for new services.

The regulatory body also must establish internal decision-making procedures that produce, to the extent possible, fair and consistent decisions. These procedures should include delegation of routine decision making to staff personnel. Some independent judicial or ministerial review of major decisions may be desirable to ensure that the regulatory agency is held accountable to established goals and objectives and to prior decisions.

Third, the entity should be organized internally along functional lines to permit maximum flexibility to adjust to market developments. Ideally, the agency should be able to establish and to restructure its own internal organization as circumstances require. Human resource policies should be aimed at attracting qualified and expert personnel who will be encouraged to stay with the entity for the duration of their careers. These personnel should be challenged with substantial responsibility and given incentives to contribute individually to the overall objectives of the agency. In the United States the Federal Communications Commission implemented a system of bonuses for extraordinary performance that resulted in high morale and great productivity.

Design of a flexible regulatory framework

Before specific regulatory policies can be adopted with respect to particular services, an overall regulatory framework should be devised. There is no perfect way to design a regulatory framework. In a market that is partially monopolistic and partially competitive, continual adjustments of the demarcation between classes of services are inevitable. Some options for classifying services are more adaptable to continued technical growth than others. Examples from industrialized countries include:

- In the United States, a distinction is made between common carriers and noncommon carriers. An additional distinction is made between basic services and enhanced services.

- Japan makes a distinction between facilities-based carriers and resale carriers. It also has two different classifications of value-added service providers.

- Germany classifies services as mandatory (monopoly), permissive, and competitive.

- France generally makes a distinction between open networks and closed networks.

- The United Kingdom maintains a classification for public telecommunications operators and several classes of special service providers.

Each of these frameworks has its advantages and drawbacks. Generally, however, regulatory frameworks that are based on classifications of operational characteristics and service definitions tend to require periodic change to accommodate different market circumstances. In addition to distinctions between classifications of services, regulatory models often classify carriers according to market power. In the United States, common carriers are either dominant or nondominant, depending on the competitiveness of the market and the size and power of the carrier.

In many administrations the basic distinction is still between the monopoly service provider (usually the Post, Telegraph, and Telephone Administration, or PTT) and services open to competition. Argentina is an example of a country that selected a monopoly model for a prescribed term. An alternative model is a duopoly structure, such as the one originally implemented in the United Kingdom in the early 1980s with British Telecom and Mercury. In March 1990 the British government announced dramatic policy changes eliminating the duopoly and opening many markets to competition. Australia also is currently considering a duopoly structure, with the privatization of Aussat. Although Japan did not institutionalize a duopoly, it has opened its markets in very measured steps, authorizing only a limited number of competitors to NTT and KDD. In contrast, Chile and New Zealand selected fully competitive markets from the start.

An alternative to a regulatory framework based on classifications of services and carriers may be a framework structured around levels of regulatory oversight, ranging from heaviest regulation to virtually no regulation. Each level would presumably include different combinations of compliance with regulatory requirements including facilities licensing, tariff review, accounting requirements and pricing policies, standard setting, and interconnection requirements. This sort of organization permits the regulatory entity to select the appropriate level of oversight based on the nature of the service provided, the market power of the carrier, and the status of competition in the market. Classifications can be shifted to suit changing circumstances without the necessity of creating revised service definitions. This approach also may be most appropriate for developing countries that do not yet have elaborate, well-established regulatory structures. Such countries need to match the level of oversight appropriate for a particular carrier with their own existing levels of regulatory resources. The success of this alternative obviously would depend on the strength and stability of the regulatory entity.

Regardless of service classifications and regulatory frameworks for determining which markets may admit competitive entry, spectrum allocation presents unique considerations. Special attention should be given to categorizing spectrum uses most suited to the needs of the country and establishing procedures for efficient and fair allocation to competing uses. Overall planning of the spectrum resource may be best centralized in an office that can be responsive to the needs of both the telecommunications and mass media sectors. The office also can ensure compliance with international requirements and accommodation of national security and other governmental needs. However, the development of service rules and the licensing of individual operators within each service spectrum allocation should be delegated to the regulatory entity. The regulatory entity also should have significant input into proceedings dealing with reallocation of spectrum. This is important to ensure that spectrum uses are allocated according to actual market requirements, rather than by centralized government planning.

Implementation of regulatory policies in transitional phases

The privatization process, including both the transactions affecting the initial disposition of assets and the process of functioning as a private enterprise, causes great dislocation and requires tremendous adjustment. Not all objectives can be achieved at once. For most countries it would be advisable to develop a transitional plan, spanning five to ten years, that would incorporate steps for steady progress toward a more competitive market.

In the initial stages of the transition, the regulatory entity must focus on strengthening the backbone network and infrastructure. This stage may require that certain basic services be provided on a monopoly basis to ensure that the proper financial incentives exist to maximize value in the privatization process and to ensure adequate development of the backbone network's capital plant. The beginning period will require the implementation of pricing policies that encourage investment, the rebalancing of tariffs to achieve more "rational" prices for use of the network, development of technical standards and network architecture for interconnection of competitive service providers, and the establishment of subsidy mechanisms to provide service to rural and high-cost areas.

An initial phase also may include authorization of certain independently provided services that do not necessarily impair the network infrastructure. Such services may include cellular systems, which can help alleviate traffic congestion, and value-added networks. The authorization of intracompany networks may also be included in this initial phase. Intracompany networks may raise questions about frequency allocation, however, particularly if the allocation table in place mirrors the U.S. distinction between common carrier and noncommon carrier operations. These issues should be resolved before intracompany networks are authorized, with the expectation that such networks ultimately may be used to provide service to third parties.

In an intermediate phase of the transition, once pricing structures have been rationalized and an investment program is well established, additional facilities-based competitors may be authorized. These competitors would include specialized networks providing service to third parties and reselling infrastructure facilities. Successful implementation of this middle phase would require that the regulatory structure be sufficiently mature to accommodate inevitable interconnection between these specialized networks and the public switched network. Such interconnection, which may be effected through private branch exchanges located on subscriber premises or through switching provided by specialized carriers to local distribution networks, is virtually impossible to detect or to prevent. The regulator must therefore have in place pricing policies that require the specialized networks to make an appropriate contribution to the cost of maintaining the local exchange. Proper implementation of these pricing mechanisms will prevent undesirable diversion of lucrative traffic from the public switched network and will support the benefits of the public infrastructure for all users.

In a final and more mature period of transition, competition may be introduced into international services. International markets are made complex by the fact that Intelsat is an international membership consortium and that it is difficult to assign Intelsat signatory responsibilities to different entities. Successful introduction of competition in international services requires that the cost of providing Intelsat space segment be separately identified and "unbundled" from end-to-end rates. Each competitor, including the Intelsat signatory, should be able to obtain space segment capacity on similar terms and conditions. International services provided through teleports or over international undersea cables may be implemented without this complication. It is difficult and inadvisable to limit carriers to the types of transmission facilities that may be used, however.

As progress toward competition is implemented through these various phases, regulation may be liberalized and eliminated. Undoubtedly in the early phases regulation must be most stringent. As pricing and technical interconnection systems are put into place to ensure the preservation of the infrastructure and as additional competitors can be accommodated, regulatory bonds may be loosened. As the network matures, classification of particular services and carriers may be changed from the most strict to more liberal levels to no regulation whatever.

Finally, it is extremely useful to build into the initial regulatory framework a specified period of review. This period of review may be used to assess carrier performance against established service objectives and to reassess the appropriateness and effectiveness of the regulatory framework established. A predetermined reevaluation point will create incentives on the part of both the industry and the regulatory entity to achieve established objectives more quickly and surely.

Conclusion

Latin American countries contemplating telecommunications privatization have a unique and important opportunity. The telecommunications infrastructure, if properly nurtured, can infuse entire economies and social structures with a new vitality and strength. Success will depend on a measured approach to the introduction of market forces. As described in this chapter, the key to this approach is the implementation of an effective regulatory framework and entity.

All participants in the privatization process should be concerned about the design of the regulatory framework and the function of the regulatory entity. For the seller, a well-designed regulatory structure will ensure that the basic telephone network is given the highest possible value and that reasonable public service obligations can be identified and carried out. For the potential purchaser, the proper regulatory structure ensures stability and the protection of investment. For competitive service providers, it defines opportunity.

Each country has its own needs and resources and will develop its own solutions. We hope that these solutions look past the initial transaction toward a broader concept of privatization. Bearing this broader concept in mind, regulatory structures can be implemented that enable each country to maximize the benefits of infrastructure for all of its citizens and to realize enhanced growth and development of the economy as a whole.

Private Participation in the Electric Power Sector

For many developed and developing countries private participation in the electric power sector can help resolve recurring problems of insufficient financing and inefficient operations. This chapter will review the power shortage problem in developing countries and what may happen over the next ten to twenty years. It will then set forth various approaches to private participation that developed and developing countries have adopted. Next comes a brief description of the requirements for effective private participation in the power sector. Finally, it reviews some of the experiences of countries around the world.

Power Shortages in Developing Countries

An adequate and reliable supply of electricity is essential for social and economic development, for both developed and developing countries. The industrial, commercial, and service sectors of the world's economies are highly dependent on this form of energy. The demand for energy in developing countries has increased more than 5.5 percent per year during

The author would like to acknowledge the contributions made to this paper by Messrs. Mangesh Hoskote, John Hammond, and William Polen. The U.S. government has the right to retain a nonexclusive, royalty-free license in and to any copyright covering this paper.

the past fifteen years, and the demand for electricity has been growing at 7 percent per year.[1]

Yet developing countries on the average use only 500 kilowatt-hours (kWh) of electricity annually per capita, compared with over 10,500 kWh per capita in the United States and 6,000 kWh per capita in Europe and Japan. More than 75 percent of the world's population consumes only 18 percent of the total electricity used (see figure 8.1).

Faced with large increases in demand, many countries now experience power shortages of over 10 percent of their generation capability. In the Dominican Republic, for example, power shortages during the past five years have been greater than 15 percent of the demand.

Two factors responsible for the current or projected power supply problems facing publicly owned utilities in developing countries are insufficient financial resources to expand power systems to keep up with the growing demand and inefficiencies in generation, transmission, and distribution.

Developing countries simply need more electric power for socio-economic development than their public sector enterprises are now able to deliver.

Effects of Power Shortages

The negative economic effect of these shortages on developing countries has been tremendous (see table 8.1). Private industry in developing countries is perhaps hardest hit by power shortages. Various studies have revealed that power outages alone can cause economic losses of approximately US$1 per kWh not supplied. In Pakistan, for example, power shortages in the industrial sector alone have led to a 1.8 percent decrease in GDP and a 4.2 percent decrease in the country's foreign exchange earnings. For India the cost to industry of the unreliable electricity supply has been estimated at 1.5 percent of gross national product (GNP).[2]

These estimates, however, do not include the value of future investments forgone because of unavailable or unreliable electric power. The installation of backup, oil-dependent diesel generator sets has been the most common solution by industrial and commercial firms for unreliable grid-supplied power. This use of diesels, however, is uneconomic since units operate only part-time, causing high capital costs per kilowatt-hour. It has been estimated that some 10 percent of the total installed generating capacity in many developing countries is in the form of standby generation on customer premises. This also diverts investment capital from other, more productive uses.

FIGURE 8.1 Distribution of World Per Capita Electricity Consumption, 1984

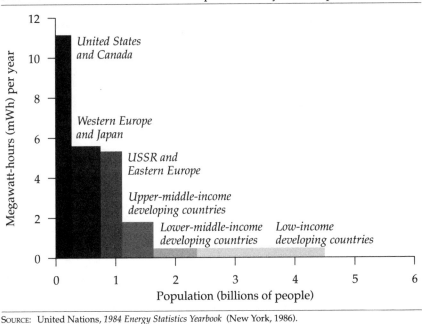

SOURCE: United Nations, *1984 Energy Statistics Yearbook* (New York, 1986).

TABLE 8.1   Costs of Power Shortages in Selected Developing Countries

Country	Sector	Cause of shortage	Shortage cost
Brazil	Household	Unplanned outage	US$1.95–3.00/kWh
Chile	Household	Unplanned outage	US$0.53/kWh
	Industry	Unplanned outage	US$0.25–12.00/kWh
Egypt	Industry	Unplanned outage	US$0.40/kWh
India	Industry	Load shedding	1% to 3% of GDP
Jamaica	Industry	Unplanned outage	US$1.25/kWh
Pakistan	Industry	Load shedding	US$0.46/kWh
Tanzania	Household		US$0.50/kWh
	Commercial		US$1.00/kWh
	Industry		US$0.70–1.40/kWh

NOTE: Load shedding is the utility practice of planned outages because of shortage of capacity.
SOURCE: Oak Ridge National Laboratory, "The Impact of Inadequate Electricity Supply in Developing Countries" (Oak Ridge, Tenn., January 1988).

Clearly, power shortages and supply failures—particularly in developing countries—disrupt productive economic activities and threaten future industrial, agricultural, and commercial investments. As demand for electricity has grown in developing countries, many governments have found it increasingly difficult to allocate sufficient resources to the power sector to meet demand—despite the fact that in many countries the power sector consumes more than 20 percent of the government's total development budget, and foreign borrowing for the power sector is often greater than 30 percent of the country's total foreign debt. Because of their financial difficulties, however, many utilities in developing countries do not qualify for loans from international development or commercial banks, making prospects for improved power supply more uncertain.

Future Power Sector Capacity and Financial Requirements

The problem is likely to become even worse in the future. In a report entitled *Power Shortages in Developing Countries*,[3] the U.S. Agency for International Development projected that if the current trend in expansion of electricity supply in developing countries continues under a modest economic growth rate of 4.5 percent per year until the year 2008, developing countries will need additional capacity for power generation of over 1,500 gigawatts (GW), compared with the 1984 installed capacity of 450 GW (see figure 8.2). This will require an annual investment of about US$125 billion per year, compared with current expenditures of about US$50 billion, necessitating a total capital investment of US$2.5 trillion.

Through dramatic improvements in the efficiency of supply and end use and with strict conservation, the need for additional generation capacity may be reduced to 700 GW during the 1988–2008 period. Nevertheless, there is a growing consensus that publicly controlled utilities—because of an inability to secure financing, a lack of spare parts, political influence, and inefficient operations—will not be able to achieve this conservation scenario.

Even if improvements in conservation and efficiency are successfully implemented, this "least-cost" strategy will require investments on the order of US$70 billion per year for new generating capacity. This portends a capital gap of about US$300 billion during the next twenty years.

For Latin America and the Caribbean, according to recent World Bank reports,[4] electricity supply is projected to grow an average of 5.4 percent per year from 1989 to 1999 (see table 8.2). This growth will require over US$155 billion in additional capital investment.

Assembling the financial resources for this level of expansion and investment is clearly beyond the capabilities of developing countries alone.

FIGURE 8.2 Projected Electricity Investment Needs for Developing Countries (Medium Growth Scenario), 1988–2008

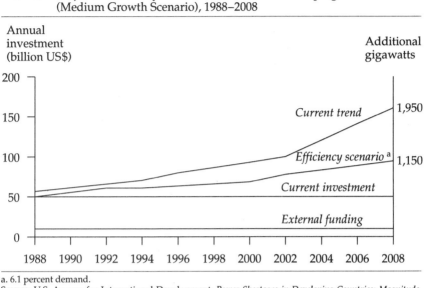

a. 6.1 percent demand.
SOURCE: U.S. Agency for International Development, *Power Shortages in Developing Countries: Magnitude, Impacts, Solutions, and the Role of the Private Sector* (Washington, D.C.: 1988).

Investment capital of this magnitude will not be available from the public treasuries of developing countries. Revenues of many, if not most, publicly owned utilities cover only a small fraction of their operating and capital expansion expenses. International development banks, such as the World Bank and the Inter-American Development Bank, and bilateral donors can supply only a small fraction of the needed capital.

System Inefficiencies

One of the major causes of the financial difficulties of publicly owned utilities is their uneconomic pricing of electricity. Some governments, for a number of social and political reasons, choose to subsidize electricity prices to all or certain groups of consumers. Almost all developing countries subsidize heavily the electricity they provide to agricultural and residential consumers. Comparison of tariff trends between OECD (Organization for Economic Cooperation and Development) countries and developing countries shows that, along with the cost of living, prices of electricity have steadily increased in OECD countries, whereas they have steadily decreased in developing countries (see figure 8.3). This decrease

TABLE 8.2   Electric Power Requirements in Latin America and the Caribbean, 1989–1999

Country	Total generating capacity required (MW)	Growth of electricity supply (average annual percentage)	Capital needs for power (million 1989 US$)	$/KW capacity added (1989 US$)
Argentina	8,535	7.0	16,237	1,902
Bolivia	369	7.0	642	1,740
Brazil	28,511	4.9	75,702	2,655
Chile	1,520	4.5	2,925	1,924
Colombia	3,026	5.7	7,759	2,564
Costa Rica	816	6.3	1,878	2,301
Dominican Republic	1,078	6.2	2,063	1,914
Ecuador	792	4.6	2,000	2,439
El Salvador	172	4.0	683	3,971
Guatemala	427	6.9	1,779	4,719
Honduras	270	7.1	579	2,144
Jamaica	309	5.2	625	2,023
Mexico	18,818	6.7	36,682	1,949
Nicaragua	35	2.0	113	3,229
Panama	120	4.4	410	3,417
Peru	1,136	5.0	3,855	3,393
Uruguay	585	3.7	1,040	1,778
Total		5.4[a]	154,972	2,592[b]

a. Average growth for the region.
b. Average amount for the region.
SOURCE: World Bank, *Capital Expenditures for Electric Power in the Developing Countries in the 1990s* (Washington, D.C., 1990).

FIGURE 8.3 Trends in Average Electricity Prices, Developing and OECD Countries, 1979–1988

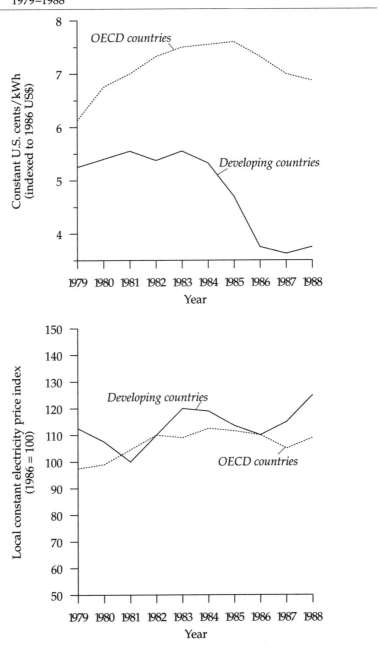

SOURCE: U.S. Agency for International Development, Office of Energy, *International Energy Agency 1988 Energy Prices and Taxes*, 4th quarter (Paris).

represents a growing disparity between actual production costs and the rates charged consumers, which are inconsistent with the requirements of the utilities for revenue. Revenues collected do not adequately cover the costs incurred in producing electricity; pricing is based on political and socioeconomic factors more than on cost accounting principles.

In some countries the amount of the subsidy to agricultural and residential consumers is staggering. In India, for example, the cost of supplying one kWh of electricity to an agricultural customer is more than 14 U.S. cents, while the customer is charged less than 3 U.S. cents.

Many publicly owned utilities in developing countries are large, entrenched institutions. They are often overstaffed, pay low salaries, and have inadequate management. One measure of institutional efficiency is the customer-to-employee ratio. In Japan, for example, this ratio is one employee to 429 customers; in the United States, the ratio is about one employee to 175 customers. In Latin America, based on recent World Bank reports, the average ratio is one employee to 89 customers (see table 8.3). This ratio is very similar to that of other developing countries, where the publicly owned utilities are required to perform social service and employment functions that often conflict with their mission to provide efficient electric service.

Many utilities in developing countries are also characterized by inefficient planning and management. In part this results from the inability of publicly owned utilities to attract and to retain a sufficient number of qualified engineers, planners, and managers. This has restricted the ability of these utilities to adopt modern least-cost system planning and dispatch techniques, energy conservation programs, and demand-management programs.

Furthermore, power supply in developing countries is characterized by low fuel-use efficiency and low capacity factors, especially for thermal plants. While typical steam plants in developed countries require 9,000 to 11,000 British thermal units (Btu) of fuel per kWh, in many developing countries the fuel requirement is over 13,000 Btus per kWh. In addition, because of the frequent breakdown of power plants and lack of proper maintenance, many power plants in developing countries have low capacity factors. In Latin America, the average capacity factor for thermal plants has been 40 percent, compared with more than 70 percent in developed countries (see table 8.3).

Another common problem is the extremely high losses of electricity in the transmission and distribution (T&D) network. While T&D losses should normally be below 10 percent of gross generation (economically optimal losses may be as low as 5 percent), the average loss in Latin America was 18 percent (see table 8.3). These losses are attributable to technical problems and unauthorized use of power—in other words, theft.

TABLE 8.3   Electric Power System Performance
in Latin America and the Caribbean, 1987

Country	Customers per employee	Total system losses[a] (%)	Capacity factor[b] (%)
Argentina	122.51	17	37
Bolivia		21	36
Brazil	119.64	19	50
Chile		17	45
Colombia	179.89	24	57
Costa Rica	94.96	10	43
Dominican Republic	92.11	30	51
Ecuador		21	34
El Salvador	175.46	14	32
Guatemala	66.36	16	27
Honduras	74.09	15	36
Jamaica	141.57	24	36
Mexico	161.17	13	47
Nicaragua	57.02	17	39
Panama	52.55	19	35
Peru	118.99	19	47
Uruguay	25.73	19	36
Venezuela	127.65	9	32
Average	89	18	40

a. Losses of electricity in the transmission and distribution network.
b. Percentage of plant availability in terms of electricity delivered.
NOTE: Blank cell indicates not available.
SOURCE: World Bank, *Summary Data Sheets of 1987 Power and Commercial Energy Statistics for 100 Developing Countries* (March 1990), p. 1.

Role of Private Participation in the Power Sector

The central theme of this chapter is that, for many developed and developing countries, private participation in the electric power sector can assist in resolving the recurring problems of insufficient financing and inefficient operations. Private participation can come in the form of independent generation plants; industrial cogeneration and self-generation with sales to the public grid; privatization of utility ownership through partial or complete sale of assets; or privatization of distinct utility services such as generation, distribution, or transmission functions through management contracting and leasing. Privatization can also mean cutbacks in government investment in power projects to allow greater participation by the private sector in ownership and operation of future power generation projects. Needless to say, no single approach is best suited for all countries.

The topic of independent, private power generation has become extremely important not only in the United States but also throughout the world. Since 1978 the United States, under the Public Utilities Regulatory Policies Act (PURPA), has seen the rapid growth of private, nonutility power generation. Nonutility generating capacity now comprises over 27,000 megawatts (MW), or 4 percent of the total U.S. generating capacity of 681,200 MW. In 1990, 30 percent of the total capacity additions for generation—over 2,800 MW—came from private investors in independent power plants (see figure 8.4).

Rationale for Private Participation

Given the poor state of the power sector in so many developing countries and given the huge financial requirement that the power sector imposes on national treasuries, more and more developing countries are looking to the private sector to help develop needed improvements and expansion in the power sector. Favorable policies toward private participation in power in Latin America have been adopted in Chile, Argentina, Costa Rica, and other countries. The reasons most often given by developing countries for increasing private sector involvement are financing, efficiency, and innovation.

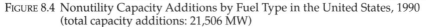

FIGURE 8.4 Nonutility Capacity Additions by Fuel Type in the United States, 1990 (total capacity additions: 21,506 MW)

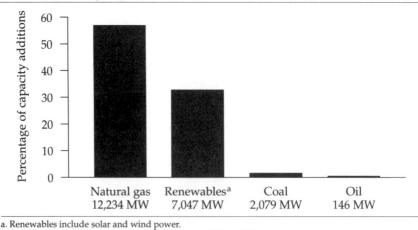

a. Renewables include solar and wind power.
SOURCE: U.S. Agency for International Development, Office of Energy.

Financing

Private investment, if it can mobilize additional sources of funds, can help alleviate the serious drain on the public treasury now imposed by the power sector. This would free up resources for expenditure in other areas such as education, health, or agriculture. It would also provide a new capital market for local private investment. A power station or stock in a utility is one of the few areas in which a major substitution of private investment for public investment can be made quickly. Also, the private sector party assumes responsibility for both equity and debt, which are then carried on the balance sheet of the private company rather than by the government or the publicly owned utility. The private sector also has access to sources of capital that are not normally available to the government-owned energy sector. This assists the governments of developing countries to expand their energy production and delivery capacity.

Efficiency

Arguments for private participation related to efficiency are rooted in the fact that many developing country utilities are state-owned monopolies where investment decisions are dictated by the monopoly supplier, with rate payers having little influence. Private participation would end this monopoly. Under the assumption that competition would dictate that profit margins of the plant depend on the efficiency of the operations, private participation would thus create savings that could be shared between the plant owner and the utility's customers.

The extent of the savings generated by private participation depends on how well the efficiency improvements counterbalance the higher cost of capital from private rather than from public sources. Capital charges per kilowatt-hour relate directly to interest rates for capital and to the number of hours per year the plant is operating. A private plant built with commercial financing at 15 percent interest would have to sell 50 percent more electricity than a plant built with 10 percent financing to have an equal capital charge per kilowatt-hour, everything else being equal.

With private participation, however, all other factors are not held equal because the private sector can introduce efficiency improvements to its power plants. Private participation can lead to rapid development of power plants and higher capacity and availability factors. This not only decreases a country's overall need for new generation, but could also reduce fuel consumption and related foreign exchange requirements. In addition, private power plants, if they were well run, would set a standard for publicly owned plants to emulate.

Privately owned and operated power companies increase the probability of management autonomy, thereby helping shield the power sector from undue political influence, which is now so prevalent. With autonomy, power system optimization becomes possible. Inefficient procurement and employment requirements can be removed.

A final efficiency-related argument is that the private sector can quickly respond to problems. Once it has government approval, it can construct new plants and transmission and distribution lines faster than the public sector and can better undertake load management and other innovative means to meet growth in demand.

Innovation

The private sector rather than the public sector has been the source of most technological and system management innovation in the power industry. With its focus on efficient operations and enhancing its rate of return, private sector firms have invested heavily in innovations in technology and system management. Private power companies are constantly seeking new measures to improve plant performance, methods such as more efficient boiler configurations, exhaust heat recovery, combined cycle gas turbines, fluidized bed combustion systems, and modular design. Private sector innovation has also led to the installation of cost-effective pollution control technologies and the design of more environmentally benign generation facilities.

Private companies have also led the way in the adoption of innovative techniques for system management. They led the move toward the use of computer technology for system planning and load forecasting, generation dispatch, and personnel management.

Approaches to Private Power

Three general approaches to private participation have been used in the power sector: independent power production, privatization through divestiture of utility assets, and utility service contract management.

Independent power production

Independent power facilities are stand-alone, privately owned and operated electric power plants that sell bulk power to the national grid. This category includes industrial or commercial cogeneration and self-generation facilities that sell to the grid.

Independent power facilities can be developed through several approaches. The most commonly discussed is the build-own-operate-transfer (BOOT) model as developed in China at the Shajiao plant and in Pakistan at the Hab River project. The Dominican Republic and Costa Rica are also following this approach. Under the BOOT scheme, private developers construct a power-generating station, sell power to the utility for an agreed-upon price, and transfer the project to the utility at a nominal price once the project debt has been repaid. A variation on this theme is build-own-operate (BOO), in which no ownership transfer takes place.

In the past, BOOT/BOO type projects have been used to finance power plants, toll roads, water supply facilities, and port facilities. These projects involve limited-recourse financing, meaning they are financed on the basis of the cash flow and risks associated with each project and not on the credit or other unrelated assets of the project owners. Creditors and providers of debt financing have only limited recourse to the project owners. These projects have tended to be complex and require detailed analysis to ensure that all risks are satisfactorily covered and that there are adequate rates of return and cash flow to attract private investment.

Debt is commonly raised by the project company from commercial sources, often with the backing of export credit guarantee agencies or multilateral or bilateral donors. Lenders are generally not covered by direct full sovereign guarantees. Debt-equity ratios are typically in the range of 70–85 percent debt and 15–30 percent equity.

All BOOT/BOO projects to date have been complex from both a legal and a financial standpoint because of the need to minimize risks to the various participants in the project. As a result they have been expensive projects to develop. The typical project agreement structure is quite complex (see figure 8.5).

The project company is typically formed by a consortium of project developers, foreign and local investors, equipment suppliers, and contractors who form a private company to build and operate the power facility. Government support has been critical in guaranteeing the performance of government entities (for example, the electric utility, national petroleum company, customs and immigration officials) and for guarantees to cover foreign exchange. Government is also responsible for removal of legal and regulatory constraints.

Privatization through divestiture of utility assets

The privatization of the electric power sector is being implemented in a number of countries in the Caribbean and Latin America. For example, the government of Argentina has authorized a restructuring of the generation, transportation, and distribution of electricity. This includes a concession

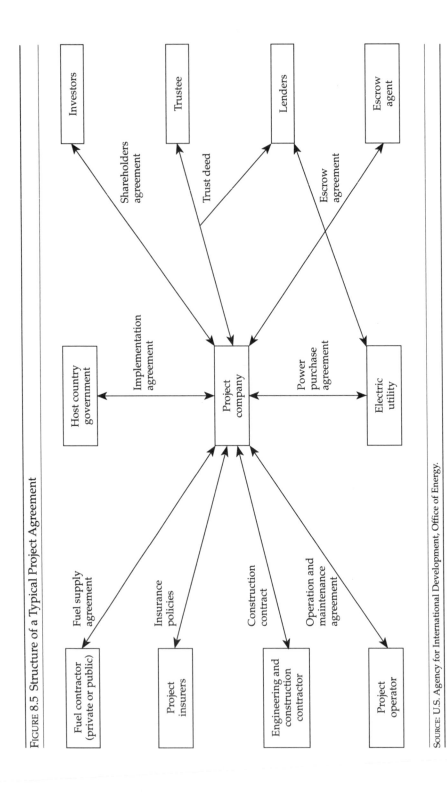

FIGURE 8.5 Structure of a Typical Project Agreement

Investors

Shareholders agreement

Trustee

Trust deed

Lenders

Escrow agreement

Escrow agent

Host country government

Implementation agreement

Project company

Power purchase agreement

Electric utility

Fuel contractor (private or public)

Fuel supply agreement

Project insurers

Insurance policies

Engineering and construction contractor

Construction contract

Project operator

Operation and maintenance agreement

SOURCE: U.S. Agency for International Development, Office of Energy.

for the distribution and sale of electricity. In addition to the Argentine privatization, other countries are also progressing. The Dominican Republic is assessing the market for potential privatization of specific municipal and electric utility services. In Chile the electric utility system has also been privatized.

Privatization of infrastructure industries such as an electric utility requires the political stamina to withstand strong counterpressures from labor unions and the general public. Because electricity is a basic input to the manufacturing sectors, the price and reliability of supply affects the international competitiveness of domestic products for export earnings. Privatization of electric utility systems must focus on improving efficiency and promoting competition for new generation plants.

Categories of privatization.   Privatization of electric utility systems can be classified into two broad categories: privatization of *electricity production* and privatization of *electricity provision*.

Privatization of electricity production means the private sector owns and operates the power plants and transmission lines and is also responsible for power delivery to the customer. This process involves total divestiture of utility assets by the government to the private sector. The British and Malaysian privatizations follow this model. Privatization of electricity production through the divestiture of utility assets involves the sale of the entire assets of the utility operations, including generation, distribution, and transmission, to a group of private investors.

Privatization of electricity provision means the private sector provides specific utility services such as operation and maintenance services for a specific power plant or a group of plants; power distribution systems including metering, billing, and collection services; security services; and fleet system management. This mode of privatization is discussed below under the heading "Utility services contract management."

Techniques of divestiture.   Divestment of state-owned entities can be facilitated by tender, auction, fixed-price offer, and management/employee buyout. Total privatization of electric utilities requires a strong commitment on the part of the government, a well-developed capital market, access to electric services for a large proportion of the population, and a utility that is in investment-grade condition. When privatizing an electric utility these factors become even more important because of the central role the utility plays in the economy. Electric utilities have traditionally been difficult to privatize. This has been due in part to the tendency of governments to use the utilities for political patronage.

The successful privatization of publicly owned utilities, however, generally requires that the utilities first be placed on a sound financial and operational footing. Efforts to privatize a company in relatively poor financial condition may not be possible since assets may be severely deteriorated, prices may not cover capital and operating costs, and operations may not be efficient.

Utility services contract management

Privatization of electricity provision by contracting out specific utility services constitutes a contractual obligation: delivery of electric service for a fee to be paid by the utility. Purchase of existing utility-generating capacity or service areas by the private sector carries the following considerations. The publicly owned utility removes the debt from its books and may obtain some foreign exchange in the process. The utility may also realize an incremental gain in capacity, either through expansion or through repowering. The private sector group is purchasing what is likely to be a proven generating unit and may lower its risks associated with construction and start-up delays. In addition, the purchase price may be low relative to new capacity additions.

The purchase and rehabilitation by private investors of an existing generation and/or distribution function is an approach being considered by many countries, including the Dominican Republic, Jamaica, El Salvador, and Panama. This would provide a cash infusion and relieve some of the foreign exchange pressures.

Electricity services are privatized through management contracts, joint ventures, and leasing.

Management contracts. A management contract is a mode of conducting business that is controlled by commercial criteria and obligations, but that does not entail the risks and benefits of ownership. In other words, a management contract is a nonequity business vehicle that facilitates the transfer of financial, managerial, and technical skills to the client and does not require direct foreign investment by either the client or the contractor. The business relationship involves three parties: (1) the client, which is the state-owned utility in the developing country, (2) a management contractor, which is the host or developed country contractor, and (3) a contract company established under the laws of the host country. Management contracting with state-owned utilities increases the potential for private sector participation in the long term. A generic structure for a utility management contract is presented in figure 8.6.

The benefits of this approach are that the private sector can reduce its up-front investment costs through contracting rather than purchasing a plant or function. The publicly owned utility is able to turn over some of

FIGURE 8.6 Structure of a Typical Management Contract

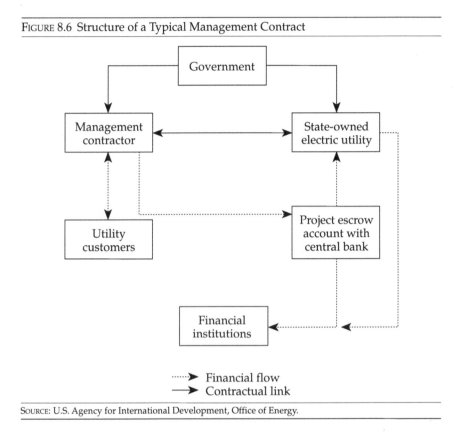

SOURCE: U.S. Agency for International Development, Office of Energy.

the maintenance and operational problems to the private sector, which can then adopt modern operational techniques and personnel practices.

Management contracting also is a low-risk market entry strategy when contractors do not have firsthand knowledge of business conditions in a developing country. Contractors gain direct experience with business culture and conditions and establish contacts with government and local businesses.

The government of Côte d'Ivoire recently signed a management contract with the French company Société Internationale de Services Publiques (SISP). Under this arrangement operation of the electric utility power stations of Energie Electrique de la Côte d'Ivoire (EECI) will be transferred to an Ivorian private-sector company, Compagnie Ivoirienne d'Electricité (CIE), in which SISP holds 51 percent of the shares (see figure 8.7). The remaining 49 percent is held by the Ivorian private sector. SISP is a

FIGURE 8.7 Structure of Côte d'Ivoire Management Contract

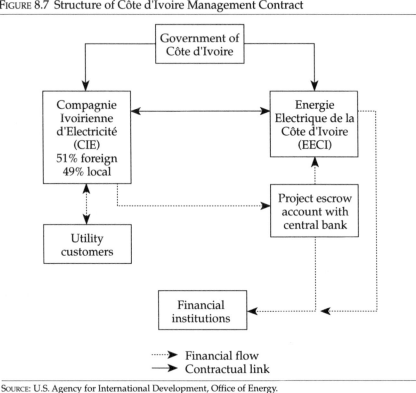

SOURCE: U.S. Agency for International Development, Office of Energy.

joint venture between a French company, SAUR Group (65 percent), and the French utility Electricité de France (35 percent).

EECI retains title to the assets of the utility. Operation, maintenance, transmission, and distribution of electricity are the responsibility of CIE. Whereas equipment replacement expenditures will be borne by CIE, future capacity expansion will be done by the government. For its electricity generation, transmission, distribution, billing, and collection services CIE receives a predetermined fee. The tariff paid by the consumers is set by the government. Any difference between the tariff and the predetermined fee is paid into an escrow account maintained at the Caisse Autonome d'Amortissement. The funds accumulated in the escrow account will be used for future capacity expansion of the utility. Planning for expansion of generating capacity will be performed by CIE, and investment decisions will be made by the government. The contract also contains adequate incentive mechanisms for efficient operation of CIE. Based on pro forma cash flow, CIE is projected to generate an annual after-tax profit equal to 2 percent of total annual sales.

Joint ventures.   A joint venture is a unique form of business association created by two parties for the purpose of engaging in a business undertaking. In the context of privatization in a developing country the joint venture provides a particularly conducive and flexible vehicle because it allows co-ownership and comanagement of the undertaking. This arrangement provides a win-win proposition because the government gains from the financial, managerial, and technical skills the private sector brings to the joint venture, and the private sector enjoys a low-risk entry into a potentially lucrative market. The joint venture offers a vehicle for achieving business and socioeconomic development objectives that may be beyond the capability of each partner acting individually. This business association also provides the concomitant benefit of sharing investment costs without exposing assets to unlimited liability.

The joint venture arrangement is not without its faults. The potential downside typically arises in the decision-making process related to management options and capital investments. To stave off potential conflicts, it is incumbent upon the joint venture partners to negotiate issues such as management structure, currency provisions, transfer pricing, dividends, repatriation, dispute resolution, choice of law, termination, representations and warranties, and force majeure.

Leasing.   Leasing is a financing mechanism whereby the state-owned utility sells a power plant to the private sector to own, maintain, and operate, and the utility in turn agrees to lease back the power plant by entering into a long-term power purchase agreement. The proceeds from the sale of the power plant are a source of income to the utility, and the private sector realizes an immediate return on its investment.

Management contracts, joint ventures, and leases can be simple first steps toward a larger role for the private sector in the utility sector. These techniques do not necessarily lead to any net additions in capacity of the utility grid, and they do not remove financial obligation for the capacity from either the government or the utility.

Requirements for Private Participation

Private participation in the power sector does not come easily. It requires new forms of public-private partnership and a sincere, long-term commitment from both sides. It also requires extensive and complex contractual arrangements. Nevertheless, the benefits appear to outweigh the costs.

The initial requirement is the sustained and fully supportive involvement of senior government officials. Without this, private sector involvement in the power sector will not take place. Numerous decisions must be made to overcome the policy, regulatory, institutional, contractual, and financial impediments that exist. While these impediments are not insurmountable, they will require the full commitment and serious attention of senior officials in the government, in the ministries of energy and finance, in the central bank, and in the publicly owned utility.

The existence of an active capital market and accounting, auditing, and security trading regulations are prerequisites for implementing a total privatization program. The domestic market must have the absorptive capacity to facilitate a stock-share distribution and purchase plan.

There is often no recent precedent for private sector participation in the power sector. A lack of knowledge and experience of how to proceed can work to delay essential decisions. While private participation in power generation offers substantial benefits, it is also a complex and difficult undertaking that requires a clear understanding of the concept and trust between the public and private sectors. Governments can benefit by learning from the experience of other countries.

Based on our analysis of the power sectors in many developed and developing countries, I will describe some of the requirements for the success of private participation.

Favorable public policy

There must be a strong, explicit public policy commitment to encourage private participation in the power sector, especially since the sector has been viewed by many as a "natural" function of the public sector. Laws and regulations should, if possible, encourage this approach, declaring that private participation is in the public interest and part of official government policy. Additionally, the public sector must be willing and able to enter into long-term contractual commitments that will enable the private sector to finance its operations. Specific financial and nonfinancial incentives are needed, such as tax holidays and exemptions and access to foreign exchange.

To attract private investment, the government should provide a public commitment of a specific amount of power to be sought in the future from the private sector. The public policy should then identify the government official who is responsible for various actions and who has final authority over the matter.

Clear regulatory and institutional framework

The government should set forth a clearly defined regulatory and institutional framework. Private investors need to know how to qualify for investments, how proposals will be solicited and evaluated, how purchase prices will be determined, and who will be responsible for making government decisions. Rules and procedures regarding independent power facilities, cogeneration facilities, management contracting, and investment in privatized utilities are essential to reduce the uncertainty faced by private investors interested in entering a sector traditionally monopolized by the government.

Formal regulatory guidelines would provide the private sector with a better understanding of how to participate with the government in supplying the nation's energy needs. The regulations should address eligibility requirements; competitive and noncompetitive solicitation procedures; methods of determining purchase price; functional and technical specifications; interconnection requirements; and procedures for resolving disputes. Clear lines of institutional responsibility must be set. Frequently governments need to establish interministerial committees since independent power and privatization actions commonly require the involvement of the ministries of finance, justice, energy, industry and commerce, and environmental control and the central bank. The publicly owned utility commonly must play a central role because of its access to information and understanding of the complexities of operating the utility system.

The authority for setting power prices and executing bona fide contracts must be clear. If the source of fuel is a government agency, this must be clarified. Someone must assume responsibility for ensuring compliance with environmental reviews and standards. And, most important, someone in the government must be responsible for ensuring the timely approval of necessary permits and clearances.

Contractual requirements

Private participation in the power sector, whether it is independent power, privatization, or management contracting, is wrapped in complex layers of mutually reinforcing contractual agreements. For independent power, the utility must execute firm contracts for the purchase of power. These must often be backed up by agreements with collateral government agencies. Fuel supply contracts, operation and maintenance contracts, insurance agreements, and many other legally binding agreements are also required for private sector participation.

Since independent power projects are typically ten to twenty years in duration, all parties must rely on the long-term sanctity of these contracts. Because of political and country financial risk, private sector investors will frequently seek to guarantee as many contractual agreements as possible to ensure against the consequences of default. The fact that the only purchaser for their product is the publicly owned utility usually will require guarantees over the life of the project, ensuring that the terms of the contract will be met.

Some of the key contractual issues that will need clarification are the following:

- How long will the contract run? Can it be extended or renewed?

- What is the purchase price, how will payments be made, and will it escalate for uncontrollable changes, such as inflation, changes in the price of fuel, and increases in labor rates?

- How will the facility be controlled and dispatched?

- Will the developer be required to transfer the facility to the publicly owned utility, or will it retain ownership at the end of the contract period?

- What are the minimal functional requirements and technical specifications for the facility?

- Who will pay for interconnection equipment? How will the accuracy of metering be ensured?

- What types of insurance will be required?

- What rights will the publicly owned utility have to monitor construction and operation?

- How will force majeure be handled?

- How will disputes be resolved?

Financial requirements

Since independent power facilities are project-financed—that is, they depend solely on the operation of the project for revenues to repay long-term debt and equity investments—these projects are supported primarily by an interlocking network of complex contractual and financial agreements. This is in contrast to public projects that rely on publicly raised revenues and external borrowing secured by a sovereign guarantee for repayment from the government.

The most serious financial requirement for independent power projects is the need to provide sufficient and secure revenues. Otherwise, private investors in both equity and debt will look elsewhere. Assuming the project generates the amount of power agreed upon, the project debt and equity investors must be completely confident that their investment will be repaid. Likewise, equity participants must be assured of an acceptable return on their equity. The repayments under the power purchase agreements with the government must be made on time and be convertible into the currencies in which the investments are denominated over the ten- to twenty-year life of the project.

Project financing without complete sovereign guarantees for the power sector is a new concept. The export credit agencies of the donor nations have been slow to enter this type of financing arrangement since there is little repayment experience from the independent power sector, especially under power purchase contracts with nations that have problems in obtaining adequate foreign currency exchange.

Project equity investors have very serious concerns regarding the repatriation of foreign exchange and the guarantee of payment terms (ensuring that a sufficient revenue stream is allowed for and that those revenues are collected). Often a major financial impediment is the need to ensure that foreign exchange is available to the project in order to pay down debt and pay a return to the equity investors.

Some of the key financial issues that must be clarified are the following:

- What are the sources of debt and equity? What interest rates and rates of return are needed?

- Who will guarantee the foreign loans made for the project?

- Who will ensure that the publicly owned utility meets its obligation to pay for power?

- Who will ensure the convertibility and repatriation of the revenues earned by the private investors?

- Who will assist the project developers to obtain needed government permits and clearances?

- Who will ensure that exemptions from taxes and duties are provided?

Conclusion

For many developed and developing countries, privatization and private participation in the electric power sector can assist in resolving the recurring problems of insufficient financing and inefficient operations. Private participation can come in many forms: independent generation plants, industrial cogeneration and self-generation, privatization of electricity production through ownership or leasing, and privatization of electricity provision through management contracting.

There is no "one-size-fits-all" model for privatization. A successful privatization process must maintain a sense of urgency and momentum and set realistic goals and deadlines. Countries that have well-developed capital markets and regulation of securities trading may choose total privatization. For a majority of the developing countries that do not have the requisite absorptive capacity in their capital markets, partial privatization techniques such as management contracts, leasing, and joint ventures may pave the way for future total privatization of state-owned utilities.

Notes

1. U.S. Agency for International Development, *Power Shortages in Developing Countries: Magnitude, Impacts, Solutions, and the Role of the Private Sector* (Washington, D.C., March, 1988).

2. Ibid.

3. World Bank, *Capital Expenditures for Electric Power in the Developing Countries in the 1990s* (Washington, D.C., February 1990).

4. World Bank, *Capital Expenditures: Summary Data Sheets of 1987 Power and Commercial Energy Statistics for 100 Developing Countries* (Washington, D.C., March 1990).

Oil and Natural Gas Privatization

Latin America's state-owned oil and natural gas sector is facing major challenges in the 1990s, but a large-scale privatization of the industry's assets appears less likely than a gradually increasing role for foreign and national private companies. The challenges reflect the need for capital, technology, and skilled personnel required to upgrade and expand activities at virtually all levels, from the wellhead to the gasoline pump. Annual investments of around US$30 billion are needed to achieve an expansion in Latin American energy production—including oil, natural gas, and electricity—equivalent to the 1970s, and half of that must come from outside sources.

While the region's oil-producing countries all have these needs, their approaches to drawing on outside help vary widely. Some, such as Mexico and Brazil, remain resolutely opposed to foreign ownership of oil and gas. Others, such as Venezuela, are resuming associations with foreign oil companies whose assets they had nationalized. And some, like Argentina, are dismantling their monopolies.

Despite these and other changes, ownership and development of Latin America's oil and gas should remain largely in the hands of state companies. More than 77 percent of the region's 1990 daily oil output of nearly 7 million barrels was produced by Mexico's PEMEX, Venezuela's PDVSA, and Brazil's PETROBRAS—all state-owned companies.

The proven ability of these three state companies—and, to a lesser degree, of a few others—to develop successfully their countries' oil and natural gas is a better guarantee of their continuing dominant role than the nationalistic drive that created them. National pride, along with the support of vested interests such as labor unions, nonetheless still provides a prop for some of the region's less efficient state companies. Pressure to improve the performance of many of these state oil companies is increasing, however, and reforms are under way.

Argentina's radical reform of state-owned Yacimientos Petrolíferos Fiscales (YPF) is likely to prove the exception since no other country with substantial production now appears ready to open itself to free competition as a way to force state companies to become more efficient. This means that privatization of the Latin American oil and natural gas sector on the whole will not involve the sell-off of state-owned assets. Instead, the private sector's role will increase largely through association with the state oil companies as partners in developing oil and natural gas resources.

Since Latin America's private sector largely lacks the expertise and the capital needed to take up the opportunities offered by association with state oil companies, private investment will continue to be mostly foreign. With the exception of Mexico and Brazil, most of the rest of Latin American state oil companies have already associated with foreign oil companies or are moving to do so under a variety of different terms. Even die-hard Marxist Cuba has recently signed exploration and production agreements with France's Total, Brazil's PETROBRAS, and others.

Latin American State Oil Companies

Latin America's state oil companies share aims that are common in the creation of national oil companies elsewhere, but, as a part of the developing world, they are also expected to act as catalysts of national economic growth, implements for social improvement, and a means by which their countries' governments can exercise political control over a basic industry.

The genesis of national oil companies is usually seen as a progressive change in the relationship between the state and the oil industry, evolving from an initial liberal period to growing government regulation and, finally, direct management. Venezuela is a classic example of this evolutionary process. Nationalism has often been the driving force, with Argentina creating YPF early in the process, while both Mexico and Brazil leapfrogged ahead.

The success rate of Latin America's state oil companies has been patchy, with most enterprises pursuing socioeconomic objectives more than profit. They have been forced to provide direct economic aid to communities in which they operate, to sell their products in the domestic market at a loss, and to make contributions to national development beyond the oil sector.

Intervention by constantly changing government administrations has led to instability for long-term planning and the existence of political appointees, cronyism, and corruption, which few state companies have been able to escape. Because of these social and political burdens, the managers of Latin American state oil companies have rarely had the freedom to optimize their own performances in pursuit of the commercial objectives of private oil companies.

An additional burden was added beginning in the 1970s, with Latin America's foreign borrowing spree, which especially involved PEMEX, PETROBRAS, and YPF. By the late 1980s the Latin American state oil sector's foreign debt had risen to close to US$30 billion.

The Crisis of the 1980s

The crash of world oil prices in 1986 and the subsequent continuing volatility in prices severely weakened most Latin American state oil companies by drastically limiting their financial capacity to maintain adequate investment levels. With income from exports slashed, a mounting debt service burden, and no alternative source of funds, the state companies were forced to make deep cutbacks in planned investments. The larger companies—PDVSA (Petróleos de Venezuela, S.A.), PEMEX, and PETROBRAS—retrenched and waited for better days to continue expansion plans.

Smaller companies, struggling to survive, were left only with the option of attracting foreign oil companies to undertake the exploration needed to maintain and to increase oil reserves and production. New liberal contracting terms were drawn up by a number of countries, including Argentina, Colombia, Ecuador, Peru, and Trinidad. Initial response was slow, reflecting a worldwide trend by major international oil companies to reduce expenditures for foreign exploration in the face of a persistent oil glut and uncertain future prices. This prompted even further liberalization of terms, which has continued into the 1990s in some countries.

Thus the crisis of the 1980s set in motion a retreat from Latin America's traditional resource nationalism to a more pragmatic approach, although the pace has been uneven from country to country, with occasional setbacks.

The Challenge of the 1990s

The outlook for Latin America's oil and natural gas sector in the 1990s has been improved by indications of a return to growth in world oil demand

and prices. This has prompted an upsurge in interest by international oil companies in exploration in the region, which should ensure continued growth in oil and natural gas reserves.

The shift toward free-market economic policies by most Latin American governments will add impetus to moves to liberalize the oil and natural gas sector. This will bring partial privatization of Argentina's YPF and Gas del Estado. Many countries have drawn up liberal contracts for exploration, which seem likely to stay in place. Venezuela is opening up to partnership with foreign oil companies. Brazil will review its constitutional ban on foreign investment in the near future. Mexico may be edging toward an eventual opening, with its decision to bring private capital into the petrochemical sector representing a possible prelude.

None of these moves implies a large-scale privatization of the region's state oil industries, but rather a reform away from absolute monopolies. There is a growing, but not yet widespread, trend toward handing over some non-core oil and natural gas activities to the private sector as state companies seek to streamline operations to improve efficiency. In most countries, governments have moved to eliminate the loss-making subsidies incurred by the state companies by increasing prices for domestic fuel.

These reforms should tend to reduce the scope of state oil company activities while at the same time strengthening the companies by eliminating or reducing many of the social and political commitments that have made them so inefficient in the past. This would represent a major step toward making state oil companies more economically viable.

Once state oil companies start to follow a more commercially oriented course, increasing opportunities for the private sector should emerge, as the companies shed peripheral activities to concentrate on more profitable core business and look for partners for expansion. This has already begun in some countries and will spread to the degree that state companies are allowed by their political masters to follow sound business strategies. The process is not likely to be fast or easy, and it requires a political determination that only a few Latin American governments have so far shown. Resource nationalism in Latin America may be down, but it is not out.

State Company Moves in the 1990s

Despite the often muddled mandates of many of Latin America's state oil companies, the practical problems of expanding their activities to achieve and maintain some degree of energy self-sufficiency or to increase exports strongly influence their approaches to the role of the private sector.

Only five of Latin America's fourteen oil-producing countries are net exporters, with the rest simply achieving or striving for self-sufficiency. Of the exporters only two, Venezuela and Mexico, have enough proven reserves to be long-term, major exporters. Lesser net exporters Ecuador, Colombia, and Trinidad are expected to experience production declines before the end of the century. Marginal exporters include Argentina and Peru; other producers, such as Barbados, Bolivia, Brazil, Cuba, Chile, Guatemala, and Suriname, cover only part of their oil needs. Mexico and Venezuela have alternately dominated Latin American oil production over most of this century. Mexico led in the early years but was overtaken by Venezuela at the end of the 1920s and resurged only in the 1980s. Mexico is likely to be overshadowed again in the 1990s and beyond as it opts for stable exports while Venezuela seeks expansion. Both countries now have approximately the same level of proven reserves of conventional oil, between 50 and 60 billion barrels, but Mexico's internal oil demand is more than 1.2 million barrels per day (b/d)—four times greater than Venezuela's. This led to a Mexican decision in the mid-1980s, which was only recently lifted, that allowed production to fall into balance with domestic consumption. Nonetheless, current PEMEX export levels of around 1.3 million b/d are expected to remain stable in the medium term, with any growth in production going to cover domestic demand, which is rising at more than 5 percent per year. (See table 9.1 for levels of production and reserves.)

TABLE 9.1	Latin American Oil Reserves and Production, 1990		
Country	Reserves (million barrels)	Production (thousand b/d)	Percentage change in production, 1989–1990
Argentina	2,280	473	+3.3
Barbados	3	1	+9.1
Bolivia	119	19	−3.5
Brazil	2,840	633	+7.0
Chile	300	20	−1.5
Colombia	2,000	445	+10.1
Cuba	100	15	−6.3
Ecuador	1,420	287	+2.9
Guatemala	36	4	+2.6
Mexico	51,983	2,633	+0.8
Peru	405	132	0.0
Suriname	27	4	+5.3
Trinidad	536	151	+1.1
Venezuela	59,040	2,118	+22.4
Total	121,089	6,935	+7.8

SOURCE: *Oil & Gas Journal* estimates.

Venezuelan production, which peaked at 3.7 million b/d in 1970, when the country exported nearly 95 percent of its output, is again on the rise following years of low levels, which reflected both the need for massive investment and political commitments as a founding member of the Organization of Petroleum Exporting Countries (OPEC). Venezuela is now expanding its exports of oil, natural gas, petrochemicals, and coal, with PDVSA emerging as a major international energy corporation.

These contrasting goals help to explain why Mexico and Venezuela have taken such different approaches to opening their oil monopolies to the private sector. PEMEX's more modest export targets dovetail with Mexico's traditional nationalism, although the company sees the need for outside capital and technology and has sought ways to bring in foreign help through innovative schemes. PEMEX is also beginning to act more like a commercial oil company, streamlining and restructuring its operations to increase efficiency and to enhance profits. This has included drawing private capital into the petrochemical sector. But the company's still-dominant financial position within Mexico and its high political profile rule out more radical departures in the short term.

PDVSA's moves to draw on foreign capital and technology to achieve its expansion goals have evoked a more pragmatic response in Venezuela, where some form of equity in oil and natural gas is now being proposed to foreign companies, including a number whose assets were nationalized in 1975. PDVSA is setting up a US$3 billion venture with Shell, Exxon, and Mitsubishi to export liquefied natural gas (LNG) to the United States. Under the terms of the venture, the foreign partners would share ownership of the natural gas used to produce the LNG. To make the project economically viable, Venezuela has reformed its tax laws, with special ventures such as the LNG project required to pay just 30 percent instead of the previous 67.7 percent in order to amortize investments. The LNG project is the first of various proposed joint ventures with foreign oil companies. PDVSA has already signed letters of intent with a number of companies for eventual associations involving development of Venezuela's huge heavy oil resources and export refineries.

Mixed Responses from Other State Companies

The responses from other Latin American state oil companies to the challenges of the 1990s have been mixed, with Argentina opting for reform and partial privatization while Brazil has banned foreign investment in oil and gas under its constitution. Other countries' approaches have ranged between the two extremes.

Despite deep-seated nationalism, a lack of success in state efforts to build up oil reserves and production has forced Colombia, Ecuador, Peru, and Trinidad to shift their approach to the private sector over the past few years. All four have eased contracting terms for foreign investment in oil exploration and production.

Argentina

The speed and depth of Argentina's radical reform of the oil and natural gas sector is made more remarkable by a tradition of resource nationalism that dates back to the 1920s. By the mid-1980s, it had become clear that a debt-ridden and inefficient state-owned YPF was unable to maintain the nation's oil self-sufficiency, let alone produce an exportable surplus. So in 1985 the administration of President Raúl Alfonsín started the current reform, providing new contract terms to attract greater foreign investment into the upstream exploration and production sector. President Carlos Menem's administration heightened the pace on coming into office in 1989 with the deregulation of the Argentine oil industry and the start of the breakup of YPF's virtual forty-year monopoly.

YPF's small, marginal fields and other YPF fields that were operated by contractors were sold as concessions to private companies. Foreign and local private oil companies have also bought 50 percent shares in some of YPF's main oil fields, and they now hold about a fifth of the country's 2 billion barrels of proven oil reserves. In 1991 Total Austral, a subsidiary of the France-based Total, obtained a production concession for the Patagonian oil field of El Huemul, reportedly offering to invest US$134 million. The agreement is in addition to two production concessions for oil and gas and for exploration the company is carrying out at the Río Chico field in Tierra del Fuego. Joint venture contracts have also been made with companies from the United States, Spain, and Italy.[1]

The objective of the reform is not to make YPF smaller, but to make the Argentine oil industry bigger, according to YPF's president, José Estenssoro.[2] He expects YPF soon to be streamlined and opened to public capital as a commercial enterprise. The aim is to create a balanced, integrated company, running on its own cash flow, paying taxes, and no longer receiving the government subsidies it needed to cover more than US$2.6 billion in losses in the past.

Brazil

In Brazil, despite former president Fernando Collor de Mello's vow to privatize the country's state-owned assets, any challenge to PETROBRAS's oil monopoly seems no nearer than the planned 1993 review of the constitution, which ratified the monopoly in the 1980s. PETROBRAS itself has been shaken by constant changes at the top, with four different presidents during the Collor administration. It has also had to battle to reduce loss-making subsidies due to low domestic prices for the 1 million b/d it sells in Brazil, and it has faced chronic labor unrest.

Nationalism and PETROBRAS's success in developing offshore oil reserves using its own technology seem to ensure that the company will continue to play a dominant role, however. Moreover, the Collor administration provided the cash-starved company with extra funds by gradually hiking domestic oil prices to reduce losses and allowing PETROBRAS to repay its foreign debt in order to seek fresh outside capital through international bond issues.

Colombia

Colombia has been the pacesetter in easing contracting terms for foreign investment. It consistently provides attractive terms and steadfastly respects its contractual obligations, making it a favored country for foreign oil investment. Recently, however, leftist guerrillas have taken up the flag of nationalism in attacking oil installations and calling for radical reforms, which the government has rejected.

Foreign oil companies account for about two-thirds of exploration in Colombia and have made major discoveries over the past ten years. The 1985 discovery of the Caño Limón field by Occidental more than doubled Colombia's reserves, while more recently the new Cusiana find—made by a consortium comprising British Petroleum (40 percent ownership), Total Compagnie Française (40 percent ownership), and Triton Energy Corporation of the United States (20 percent ownership)—is now expected to double them again to around 4 billion barrels. (Colombian law provides for 60 percent control of the field by state-owned Ecopetrol, with the remaining control going to the consortium.) As a result of such discoveries, Colombia's oil production has grown since the mid-1980s, making it a substantial net exporter.

Ecuador

Ecuador's approach has been ambivalent, with the administration of President Rodrigo Borja initially moving to reverse a previous policy that favored foreign oil investment and strengthening the role of state-owned Petroecuador through the takeover of some foreign oil companies' activities. But Petroecuador's lack of success in replenishing falling reserves has forced the Borja government to offer new areas to foreign firms.

In 1991 the government reached agreement on a joint venture for the production of heavy crude in the Amazon with a consortium consisting of

U.S.-based Conoco, which controls 35 percent of the project; Overseas Petroleum and Investment Corporation, a Taiwanese company; and four North American–based companies, Maxus Ecuador Inc., Noneco Ecuador, Murphy, and Canam Offshore. The venture will require approximately US$700 million in investment for drilling.[3]

The return of a more liberal administration in Ecuador's 1992 presidential elections has prompted a renewed opening for foreign oil companies and a reduced role for Petroecuador.

Peru

In Peru, President Alberto Fujimori's plans call for the opening of downstream refining and marketing activities to the private sector. PetroPerú would be left with core exploration and production activities, along with foreign oil companies.

Peru's political uncertainty and a past history of nonfulfillment of contractual obligations has left the field open to only the very brave "elephant hunters" seeking major finds in remote areas, however. One such discovery, the giant Camisea gas and condensate find made by Shell, has yet to be developed because of contractual disputes with Shell.

Trinidad

The growth of Trinidad's state oil activities has been a result of circumstance as much as an upsurge in nationalism. In fact, the takeover of the country's loss-making refining activities came as part of a settlement of claims with foreign oil companies. Trinidad has improved terms for exploration by foreign companies and has attracted a number of newcomers. It has also received financing from the Inter-American Development Bank to increase recovery of oil from old fields and to upgrade refineries.

Bolivia

Bolivia's moves to open the country to foreign oil companies have turned the country into an exploration "hot spot," but they have also prompted political controversy. State-owned Yacimientos Petrolíferos Fiscales Bolivianos (YPFB) has sweetened terms by offering existing geophysical data on different areas to foreign firms for reinterpretation and allowing new seismic surveys before committing companies to costly exploratory drilling. A March 1991 agreement between YPFB, Texaco, and Sun Oil provides for exploration and production in Chuquisaca department, with an estimated seven-year investment of US$25 million and production between 30,000 and 60,000 b/d. In February 1991, ESSO Exploration of Bolivia won a thirty-year exploration contract for the Poopo region in Oruro and La Paz departments; investment and exploration costs are expected to reach US$40 million.[4]

Chile

In Chile, production has steadily fallen in recent years, despite the efforts of state-owned Empresa Nacional del Petróleo (ENAP), and imported oil now meets the bulk of domestic demand. Proposals for the partial privatization of ENAP have run into opposition and, meanwhile, the company is continuing to assign risk contracts to foreign companies.

Small Producers and Have-nots

Cuba's decision to open the country's offshore areas to foreign oil companies is one of the most striking examples of how ideology is being replaced in Latin America by a pragmatic approach to resolving oil supply problems. Once a distant outpost of the Soviet empire, Cuba must now find a new source of supply to cover the island's requirements of approximately 200,000 b/d. Cuba's own efforts to develop resources with Soviet help met only a fraction of its needs.

Guyana has attracted oil exploration activities by several foreign companies. These include the London and Scottish Marine Oil Company (LASMO); U.S.-based Hunt Oil, which is exploring the Takutu River basin; and Mobil Oil, whose 7,700-square-mile concession on the northeast coast is equal to almost a tenth of Guyana's national territory. Guyanese gasoline and petroleum product imports are currently equal to 37 percent of the country's gross domestic product (GDP).[5]

Throughout the Caribbean and Central America, as well as farther south in Suriname, Paraguay, and Uruguay, foreign oil companies are finding their appetites for exploration whetted by increasingly liberal terms. Ironically, Venezuela, which is just beginning to open its monopoly to foreign companies, has been a major influence in promoting liberal contract terms for exploration and production in Central America. Venezuelan experts, in combination with the Latin American Energy Association (OLADE), have drafted model contracts that have been adopted by Honduras, Panama, Costa Rica, and Nicaragua.

More recently, Venezuela has signed technical agreements with Guatemala and Honduras to help do preliminary geophysical work to identify the two countries' offshore oil potential. Venezuela's promotion of exploration in Central America and the Caribbean is in its own interest because any increased or new oil production would ease its own commitments to supply the region with oil. Since the mid-1970s, first alone and then (since 1980) in tandem with Mexico, Venezuela has been providing up to 160,000 b/d of oil to nine regional consuming states under concessional terms.

Conclusion

The varying responses of the Latin American oil-producing countries to unstable oil prices, an oil glut, and domestic distractions such as mounting debts have shown that the region is unlikely to turn to wholesale privatization of the state oil companies. Instead, gradually increasing foreign participation in countries such as Venezuela, Argentina, Colombia, Ecuador, Peru, Trinidad, Bolivia, and even Cuba is a more likely herald of future trends. So too is the move toward a somewhat increased role for domestic private involvement. These changes will help bring the necessary investment, technology, and skilled personnel to improve efficiency and performance of the region's state-owned oil sector.

Notes

1. "Argentina: French Company Obtains Oil Production Concession," *Chronicle of Latin American Economic Affairs* (March 28, 1991); and "Argentina: On Partial Privatization of State-run Oil Company," *Chronicle of Latin American Economic Affairs* (August 20, 1991).

2. José Estenssoro, interview with author.

3. "On Petroecuador's Joint Venture with Conoco-Headed Consortium for Heavy Crude Production in Amazon Region," *Chronicle of Latin American Economic Affairs* (August 22, 1991).

4. "Bolivia: Texaco and Sun Oil Obtain Oil Exploration and Production Concession," *Chronicle of Latin American Economic Affairs* (March 26, 1991).

5. "Guyana: Report on Oil Exploration by Foreign Companies," *Chronicle of Latin American Economic Affairs* (April 18, 1991).

Privatization of Tourism and Air Transportation

Tourism and air transportation are two of the most vital parts of the global economy. Recent movements in Latin America and the Caribbean toward the privatization of air transportation and tourism (principally hotels) may help create a tourism industry that is more productive, committed to greater quality, and likely to be more profitable.

The growth of quality tourism (and the emphasis on privatization in this sector) is indicative of the changes taking place in the productive economic system worldwide. The goods-producing sector no longer predominates; services do.

The services sector and trade in services include diverse and fast-growing activities such as tourism, engineering, consulting, banking, transportation, motion pictures, insurance, franchising, construction, advertising, and telecommunications. Many developing countries have come to recognize that they must capitalize on their comparative advantage in international trade in services in order to maintain or to improve their competitive edge in the global marketplace. Two of the service sectors

The principal authors of the paper are David L. Edgell, Sr., and Wanda Barquin, with editorial assistance from Jean Arey and computer production by Sara Rios (Office of Policy and Planning, United States Travel and Tourism Administration). The views expressed in this text are those of the authors and do not necessarily represent those of the U.S. Travel and Tourism Administration, the U.S. Department of Commerce, or the U.S. government. Needless to say, any errors or omissions are the responsibility of the authors.

most important to developing countries in this regard are tourism and air transportation. These services have thus become part of new strategies to promote privatization and foreign investment.

Tourism and air transportation are inherently linked in that much of tourism is dependent on air transportation (especially long-haul destinations). Developments affecting the international airlines have a tremendous effect on the movement of tourists and their use of services such as hotels, resorts, restaurants, taxis, buses, recreational vehicles, attractions, convention centers, entertainment, and rental cars. Thus, while this chapter has a special focus on tourism, the transportation issues and related industry segments have been reviewed as they pertain to an overall strategy of privatization.

Policy makers have good reasons for a new focus on tourism in the 1990s.[1] The World Travel and Tourism Council, in its report *Travel and Tourism: The World's Largest Industry*, provides a clear capsule of the reasons for increased worldwide interest in tourism and air transportation.[2]

- Travel and tourism comprise the world's largest industry.

- Travel and tourism generate about US$3.5 trillion in gross output, which is 6.1 percent of world gross national product (GNP).

- Travel and tourism employ 127 million people worldwide, or one in every fifteen employees.

- Travel and tourism invest more than US$350 billion a year in new facilities and capital equipment, or 6.7 percent of worldwide capital investment.

- Travel and tourism contribute more than US$300 billion in direct, indirect, and personal taxes each year, approximately 6 percent of total tax payments.

- Travel and tourism are growing faster than the world economy in terms of output, value added, capital investment, and employment.

Some recent research suggests that during the decade of the 1990s global tourism will be the fastest growing sector in the world economy.[3]

Information from the World Tourism Organization, as presented in table 10.1, suggests that worldwide tourism arrivals increased by 58 percent from 1980 to 1991 and that tourism receipts increased by 156 percent during the same period. For Latin America and the Caribbean, arrivals increased by 53 percent, and receipts increased by 77 percent.

TABLE 10.1   International Tourism Worldwide and in Latin America and the Caribbean, 1980–1991

Year	World arrivals (thousands)	Americas arrivals (thousands)	Share of world arrivals (%)	World receipts (million US$)	Americas receipts (million US$)	Share of world receipts (%)
1980	286,474	26,011	9.08	101,020	11,813	11.69
1981	288,268	25,357	8.80	102,670	12,931	12.59
1982	287,469	24,472	8.51	96,927	9,781	10.09
1983	291,843	25,926	8.88	97,705	9,583	9.81
1984	319,230	27,802	8.71	109,004	10,575	9.70
1985	328,665	27,912	8.49	115,426	11,550	10.06
1986	339,842	29,992	8.82	139,282	12,597	9.04
1987	365,576	31,779	8.69	170,863	13,928	8.15
1988	392,578	33,740	8.59	196,809	15,052	7.65
1989	426,567	35,746	8.38	209,733	16,284	7.76
1990	454,143	39,184	8.63	253,531	19,383	7.65
1991	453,325	39,789	8.78	258,984	20,928	8.08

NOTE: Data in this table are 1991 revised estimates.
SOURCE: World Tourism Organization.

While the comparatively small increase in receipts for Latin America and the Caribbean was disappointing (and the reasons for this poor performance are not yet fully understood), future opportunities definitely exist. The Americas offer great potential for dramatic increases in tourism, but only if major improvements in policies, products, and systems take place within this decade. Other information from the World Tourism Organization indicates that, for the most part, those countries of the world whose tourism sectors are highly privatized received the most gains from tourism in the past ten years. This suggests a strong incentive for the countries of the Americas to take every opportunity to privatize their respective tourism sectors, with the likely outcome a more competitive and higher quality tourism product.

Criteria for Privatization of Tourism and Air Transportation

Privatization proposals in the tourism sector should take into consideration the specific features of the economies in which the privatization process takes place. Special attention should be given to the scale of the privatization, the level of distortion in the capital markets, the extent of the local entrepreneurial culture, and the degree of investor confidence. The transfer of the means of production from the public sector to the private domain, especially in the tourism sector, should include steps to deregulate, to decentralize, and to foster competition and market-oriented mechanisms in order to achieve an optimal state divestiture.

Significant impediments to the development of tourism include investment-related problems such as inadequate financing, ambivalence toward direct private foreign investment, and a lack of incentives for domestic investment. Additional problems include a lack of infrastructure and inadequate air access to tourism destinations.[4] Furthermore, tourism suffers in many countries from a lack of policy attention at the highest levels of government and industry, and there is often very little recognition of tourism's value to economic development and national income, and as a foreign exchange earner. As a consequence, tourism policy (and concurrently tourism privatization) in the Americas needs to be nurtured.

The three pillars of the U.S. Latin American policy referred to as the Enterprise for the Americas Initiative—trade, investment, and debt (debt reduction and debt equity)—apply directly to tourism and the process of privatization. The implementation of this policy in the tourism sector would attempt to reduce barriers to trade in tourism to improve the climate for tourism investment opportunities, and to allow for the possibilities of debt-equity and debt-for-nature swaps, all of which support private sector initiatives. It is too early to determine whether such policies will be applied to the tourism industry, but the foundation has been laid.

The restructuring of public sector enterprises, particularly the privatization of the tourism sector, involves the development of a new set of policy guidelines that could solve some of the problems faced in tourism development. Privatization efforts in tourism are so new that a new policy framework is required that would be geared not only to transferring public sector enterprises to the private domain, but also to fostering deregulation, open skies negotiations, decentralization, competition, and market-oriented mechanisms in order to create an optimal state divestiture of the tourism industry.

Increased involvement of the private sector through the total or partial sale of tourism-transportation assets previously owned by the state is only one instrument in the successful development of a more rational economic environment in which to foster profitable growth strategies for tourism. As some economists have argued, "privatization of public enterprise(s), in both developing and developed economies, proceeds from the postulate that private ownership implies more efficient production, ceteris paribus."[5] If the purpose of privatization is to allocate a limited number of resources more efficiently, it follows that private enterprises should be motivated by market signals, including the easy and clear access to information, a reduction in bureaucratic barriers to travel, and the development of strategies to maximize profits.

Advantages and Disadvantages of the Privatization of Tourism

Privatization in the field of tourism in Latin America and the Caribbean is just beginning. Privatization is not a panacea for the tourism problems of any specific country but rather is just one step in a larger strategy to increase the economic development of the region.

Some of the advantages of privatization might include

- fiscal efficiency
- allocative effectiveness
- increased productivity
- greater competition
- improved policy making
- improved quality management

- reduced pressure on governments to provide financing
- encouragement of greater public participation in the sector
- increased creativity and innovation
- greater quality of tourism products

Possible disadvantages of privatization include

- reduction of certain social goals important to the nation as a whole
- less stimulus for competition in parts of the tourism industry
- potential for development of private monopolies or duopolies, which don't necessarily provide economic efficiency
- disregard for the environment in some cases
- elimination of or lack of services (particularly air service) critical to small communities because of inadequate economies of scale

The Progress of Privatization

A conducive economic environment, including instruments such as legislative changes, a viable capital market, and coherent macroeconomic policies, is needed to support the liberalization and rationalization of the economy in developed and developing countries that seek privatization of the tourism sector. While in many respects Mexico and Jamaica have led the way in privatization of tourism and air transportation, other countries have made progress or are seeking to move in the direction of privatization. Particularly with respect to air transportation, we have seen the sale of state airlines in Argentina, Chile, Guatemala, and other countries, with programs under way to sell state carriers in Panama, Uruguay, and elsewhere in the Americas. Table 10.2 shows the progress of airline privatization in Latin America. Many countries in Latin America have taken measures to privatize their tourism industries.

Jamaica

By 1991, as part of a broad divestment program, the government of Jamaica had sold fourteen state-owned hotels to local and foreign investors. Only the Wyndham Rose Hall, a 508-room hotel in Montego Bay, is wholly owned by a foreign operator (Trammel Crow). The Mallards Beach Hotel and the Divi Americana in Ocho Rios were sold to a joint partnership

TABLE 10.2   Airline Privatizations in Process and Completed, 1991

Country	Company	Status
Argentina	Aerolíneas Argentinas	Sold 11/21/90 for US$260 million
Bolivia	LAB	Majority ownership to be sold
Chile	LAN-Chile	Sold in 1989 for US$42 million
Cuba	Cubana de Aviación	Negotiations reportedly held with Brazil's VASP
Ecuador	Ecuatoriana de Aviación	49% of shares sold in March 1991
Guatemala	Aviateca	75% of shares sold in 1989
Honduras	Tan	40% to be sold
Jamaica	Air Jamaica	To be privatized
Mexico	Compañía Mexicana de Aviación	Sold 8/22/89 for US$140 million
Mexico	Aeroméxico	Sold in December 1988 for US$400 million
Mexico	Aeronaves de México	Sold 6/12/89
Panama	Panama Air	Sold in August 1991
Paraguay	Líneas Aéreas Paraguayas	To be privatized
Peru	AeroPeru	To be privatized
Uruguay	PLUNA	To be privatized or demonopolized
Venezuela	VIASA	60% of shares sold to foreign companies, 20% to employees, under August 1991 agreement

SOURCES: *Latin Finance; AmericaEconomia: Estrategia;* USAID; *Chronicle of Latin American Economic Affairs; Hemisfile.*

between local and foreign investors, and the Royal Caribbean was also sold to a local-foreign joint ventureship. All the other properties have been sold to Jamaican entrepreneurs (see table 10.3). Other properties approved for privatization by the government include the Milk River Hotel and Spa, the Bath Fountain Hotel in St. Thomas, Jamaica Pegasus (partially government-owned), the Forum Hotel Complex, and the Oceana Hotel.[6] Furthermore, Jamaica is seeking to sell the government-owned airline, Air Jamaica, as another step in its privatization efforts.

Mexico

According to Jacques Rogozinski, director of Mexico's privatization program, the main objectives pursued in the divestiture of state-owned enterprises in Mexico were

- to decrease the size of its structure and to improve the efficiency of the government as an economic regulator

TABLE 10.3 Jamaican Hotels Privatized, 1987–1991

Hotel	Sale price (million US$)	Room occupancy	Date of sale	Buyers
Sandals Royal Caribbean	8.9	168	1987	Jamaican and foreign investors
Casa Monte	0.9	22	8/19/89	Jamaica National Building Society
Casa Montego	4.1	129	8/21/89	Jamaican investors
Inn on the Beach	1.3	47	7/12/89	National Commercial Bank and other Jamaican investors
Montego Inn	0.5	30	July 1989	Jamaican investors
Wyndham Rose Hall	22.0	500	8/1/89	U.S. Wyndham Hotel Group
Eden II	10.0	280	8/4/89	Life of Jamaica
Jamaica Jamaica	16.0	268	8/25/89	Life of Jamaica and Linval Ltd.
Hedonism II	21.5	268	9/15/89	Mutual Life and Village Resort
Trelawny Beach	10.2	350	10/3/89	Mutual Life and Village Resort
Jack Tar	7.0	128	6/15/90	Jamaican investors
Wyndham New Kingston	8.1	400	1/19/91	Jamaican investors
Mallards Beach	16.0	400	March 1991	Jamaican and foreign investors
Americana Hotel	11.0	350	March 1991	Jamaican and foreign investors
Total	137.5	3,340		

SOURCES: National Investment Bank of Jamaica (NIBJ); National Hotels and Properties Limited (NHP).

- to generate savings for the government by eliminating government subsidies and other related expenditures

- to promote increased productivity in the industrial sector by giving the tasks of production to the private sector in order to meet the new strategy for industrial reconversion and to open markets to foreign competition

These objectives have been largely met in Mexico's tourism sector.

During the first phase of the tourism sector's privatization, the Mexican government disengaged itself from nineteen hotel enterprises and from two of its aviation companies (Aeroméxico and Compañía Mexicana de Aviación). Even though the Mexican government no longer owns a majority interest in these airlines, it retained some ownership of Aeroméxico and 40 percent of the stock of Mexicana. Twenty percent of Aeroméxico has been bought by Banco Nacional de México—which itself was owned two-thirds by the government before it was sold in 1991. The Mexican government thus maintains significant influence in this sector.

The government of Mexico continues to welcome private participation in the financing of infrastructure projects and services in the tourism sector. The "New Regulation of the Law of Foreign Investment," published in 1989, liberalizes foreign access to investment in the Mexican equity market. (See table 10.4 for Mexican tourism privatizations.)

The Mexican experience in the sale of state-owned enterprises has been largely satisfactory and will encourage wider participation of national and foreign private investors in the tourism industry.

Venezuela

In August 1991, the Venezuelan government agreed to sell 60 percent of the shares in the state-owned airline, Venezolana Internacional de Aviación,

TABLE 10.4	Privatizations of Mexican Tourist Enterprises in Process and Completed, 1991
Enterprise	Status
Hotel El Mirador, S.A.	Privatized 2/8/89
Sur del Pacífico, S.A.	Privatized 5/30/90
Operadora Ex-convento de Santa Catalina, S.A.	Privatized 12/7/90
Nacional Hotelera de Baja California, S.A.	To be privatized
Recromex, S.A. de C.V.	To be privatized
Terrenos Recreo, S.A.	To be privatized

SOURCE: *Latin Finance.*

S.A. (VIASA), to a consortium headed by Spain's Iberia for US$145.5 million. Venezuela also plans to privatize a number of hotels.[7]

Chile

In 1989, the government of Chile sold LAN-Chile for US$42 million to a domestic investor and to the Scandinavian company SAS, which has also invested in Continental Airlines of the United States. The Chilean government retained 22 percent of the company's shares.[8]

Guatemala

Aviateca, Guatemala's national airline, was privatized in 1989. Under a restructuring program, 30 percent of the company's US$17.8 million authorized capitalization was acquired by Taca Airlines of El Salvador, with the government keeping a minority participation and 45 percent of the remaining shares going to domestic investors, including employees.[9]

Bolivia

In 1991 the government of Bolivia passed a decree authorizing the sale of sixty enterprises owned by the country's nine regional development corporations. Included in the sixty companies to be sold are two hotels, the Hotel Asahi in Santa Cruz and the Hotel Terminal in Oruro, and the domestic airline Línea Aérea Imperial, owned by the Potosí regional development corporation. The new legislation also provided for the government to sell shares in the national airline, Lloyd Aéreo Boliviano (LAB); several foreign airlines, reportedly including Spain's Iberia, Brazil's Varig, Hapag-Lloyd, and a Japanese consortium, have made offers for a joint venture with LAB or an outright purchase.[10]

Argentina

Argentina's privatization law 23,696, passed in August 1989, provided for the privatization of the state-owned Aerolíneas Argentinas and the wholly owned Operadora de Servicios Turísticos, S.A. (OPTAR) and for the sale of a 55 percent share in Buenos Aires Catering, S.A. Under the conditions of the award, the airline had to be sold to a group of buyers that included an international airline company larger than Aerolíneas Argentinas; no single buyer could hold more than 30 percent of the stock; and foreign participation was limited to less than 50 percent. The enterprise was purchased in November 1990 by a consortium that included Iberia Líneas Aéreas de España, S.A.; Devi Construcciones, S.A.; Cielos del Sur, S.A.; and four individual investors. A subsequent restructuring left ownership as follows: Iberia (30 percent), a Spanish investment group (19 percent), Devi Construcciones (17 percent), Amadeo Riva (17 percent), and a local investor (2 percent). Of the remaining 15 percent, 5 percent was retained by the state, while 10 percent was owned by the enterprise's 10,000 employees, who were transferred to the new enterprise. The price was US$130 million in cash, another US$130 million to be paid over ten years with a five-year grace period, and US$2.01 billion in public external debt securities. In addition, the buyers were required to invest US$684 million in the enterprise, including purchasing fifteen new airplanes, within five years after the sale. The exchange led to a US$34 million reduction in Argentina's annual deficit.

In addition to the sale of Aerolíneas Argentinas, other privatizations have taken place or are in progress in Argentina's tourism industry, at both the national and the provincial level. These include:

- Hotel Llao-Llao. Previously under the control of the National Parks administration, the hotel was sold in 1991 for US$6.24 million to a consortium comprising Citicorp, Choice, Cofipa, and Surhotel.

- Hotel Sierras de Alta Gracia. Owned by the province of Córdoba, the hotel was to be sold or awarded as a concession.

- Línea Aérea Provincial (ALFA). The province of Chaco is selling its provincial airline.

- Servicio Turístico Catamarán Caburei. The province of Misiones offered this enterprise for sale in December 1990. The province has continued efforts to sell the enterprise.

- Hotel Pilmayquén. Located in San Carlos de Bariloche in Río Negro province, the hotel was put up as a concession in May 1991. The estimated investment for the project was US$300,000.[11]

Ecuador

In March 1991 the government announced the sale of 49 percent of the shares of the state-owned airline Ecuatoriana de Aviación. The buyers included both domestic and foreign investors.[12]

Conclusion

With proper infrastructure, good transportation, adequate communications, and a strong will to improve the tourism industry, many more privatizations can be successful in the countries of the Americas. Each country must weigh the costs and the benefits and must develop special strategies for privatization, but if these steps are successfully accomplished, the countries will be able to realize significant future growth and development in tourism and air transportation.

The next few years will be critical to this process as the tourism industry demands more quality tourism products. To improve that quality and to become more competitive, the industry will become more oriented toward the private sector. Countries that expect to compete will recognize the importance of privatization in air transportation and in tourism.

Notes

1. The information contained in this section is from *Travel and Tourism: The World's Largest Industry* (Brussels: World Travel and Tourism Council, April 8, 1991). This policy-related document, based on a comprehensive study, highlights the significance of tourism in the global economy. The World Travel and Tourism Council (WTTC) is a global coalition of chief executive officers from all sectors of the industry including transportation, accommodation, catering, recreation/cultural, and travel services activities. Its goal is to promote the expansion of travel and tourism markets and encourage quality service to consumers. For further information, contact: World Travel and Tourism Council, Chaussée de La Hulpe, 181 Box 10, 1170 Brussels, Belgium. Much of the information and concepts about tourism in this chapter, and including this referenced quotation, are based on the book by David L. Edgell, Sr., *International Tourism Policy* (New York: Van Nostrand Reinhold, 1990).

2. World Travel and Tourism Council, *Travel and Tourism: The World's Largest Industry*; see also David L. Edgell, Sr., and Ginger Smith, "Tourism Milestones for the Millenium: Projections and Implications of International Tourism for the United States through the Year 2000," paper prepared for the "International Forum on Tourism to the Year 2000: Prospects and Challenges," World Tourism Organization Conference, Acapulco, Mexico, October 22–23, 1992.

3. An excellent source of information, statistics, and policies regarding global tourism is the World Tourism Organization located in Madrid, Spain, with 103 member countries in 1990. It provides an international clearinghouse for the collection, analysis, and dissemination of technical information on tourism. It offers national tourism administrations and organizations a framework for a multinational approach to international discussions and negotiations on matters concerning tourism.

4. For more information regarding this aspect of tourism, see Organization of American States, *The Development of Tourism: Latin America and the Caribbean in the Decade of the 1990s* (Washington, D.C., 1991).

5. A more detailed treatment of this subject is contained in R. McComb and J. H. Welch, "Public Enterprise and Privatization in a Duopoly Model: The Implications of Differential Costs," unpublished, 1990.

6. National Investment Bank of Japan, "Enterprises/Assets/Activities Approved for Privatization Preliminary Assessment," unpublished, 1991.

7. According to *Latin Finance*, the Venezuelan hotels and tourist enterprises to be privatized are: Caztor, Desarrollo Turístico Río Chico, Doral Beach, Eurobuilding Caracas, Hotel Aguas Calientes, Hotel Barquisimeto Hilton, Hotel Bella Vista, Hotel Caracas Hilton, Hotel Cumanagoto, Hotel Cumboto, Hotel El Tam, Hotel Humboldt, Hotel Macuto Sheraton, Hotel Maracay, Hotel Meliá Caribe, Hotel Meliá Puerto La Cruz, Hotel Miranda, Hotel Prado Río, Hotel Trujillo, Intercontinental del Lago, Intercontinental Guayana, Intercontinental Valencia, Marina de Caraballeda, Marina de Cumán, Módulo Turística de Puerto Piritu, Parque Safari Margarita, Posada Turística de Sanare, and Teleférico de Caracas.

8. "Del Cielo al Suelo," *AméricaEconomía* no. 47 (January/February 1991), pp. 22–23.

9. U.S. Agency for International Development Mission to Guatemala; "Privatizaciones: En el Eje de las Nuevas Reformas," *Estrategia* (March 18, 1991), p. 36; announcement by Latin American Financial Services Corp. (LAFISE), *Latin Finance*, supplement (March 1991), p. 10.

10. Information on privatization in Bolivia was provided by the U.S. Embassy in La Paz.

11. Information for this section is from Vittorio Orsi, *Avance de los Procesos de Privatización* (Buenos Aires: Secretaría de Planificación, July 12, 1991) and José Roberto Dromi, *Privatizaciones en Argentina* (Buenos Aires: Ministerio de Obras y Servicios Públicos, December 1990).

12. "Privatizaciones: En el Eje de las Nuevas Reformas," p. 23.

ABOUT THE CONTRIBUTORS

Paul H. Boeker is president of the Institute of the Americas. Before joining the Institute, he was a member of the U.S. Foreign Service, where his diplomatic career spanned twenty-seven years, including service as U.S. ambassador to Bolivia (1977–1980) and to Jordan (1984–1987). His other posts included director of the Foreign Service Institute and senior deputy assistant secretary of state for economic and business affairs. In 1985 he received the Presidential Distinguished Service Award from President Reagan. Ambassador Boeker is a member of the Council on Foreign Relations and the American Academy of Diplomacy. He is the author of *Lost Illusions: Latin America's Struggle for Democracy* and the introduction and epilogue to a 1991 issue of Henry L. Stimson's *American Policy in Nicaragua*. He graduated magna cum laude from Dartmouth College and received his M.A. in economics from the University of Michigan, Ann Arbor.

Wanda Barquin works as a policy analyst at the U.S. Travel and Tourism Administration, Department of Commerce. Before joining the U.S. government, she worked for almost ten years in the tourism field, accumulating experience in the airline, travel, and hospitality industries both in the United States and overseas. She conducted her undergraduate studies at the Georgetown University School of Foreign Service, where she graduated Phi Beta Kappa and magna cum laude. In 1991 she received a master's degree in Latin American studies from Georgetown University.

David L. Edgell, Sr., is senior executive director and director of the Office of Policy and Planning, U.S. Travel and Tourism Administration, for the

U.S. Department of Commerce in Washington, D.C. He is also adjunct professor of business and tourism at The George Washington University and is a charter member of the International Academy for the Study of Tourism. He is also author of the popular book on tourism entitled *International Tourism Policy* (1990).

Juan Foxley Rioseco is the vice president of finance for CORFO, the National Development Bank of Chile. Previously he has held positions with the Compañía Chilena de Inversiones; Inversiones Pocuro; Derco-Promac, Sodimac, and Friosur Holding; and Derco, S.A. He has served as a consultant for the United Nations, the Inter-American Development Bank, and the World Bank. He has served as assistant professor at the Pontificia Universidad Católica de Chile, the Universidad Católica de Valparaíso, and Instituto de Estudios Bancarios. He is the author of numerous articles and working papers on macroeconomics and finance. He received a bachelor's degree in commercial engineering, a master's degree in monetary and fiscal economics from the Universidad de Chile, and a master's degree in econometrics and corporate finance from the University of Pennsylvania, and he has done work in finance at the Wharton School at the University of Pennsylvania.

Mark S. Fowler is senior communications counsel for the law firm of Latham & Watkins. The Latham & Watkins Communications Group, based in Washington, D.C., has advised companies and governments in Europe, Latin America, Asia, and the Pacific Rim with respect to transactions and regulatory changes in connection with telecommunications liberalization and privatization. Mr. Fowler was chairman of the U.S. Federal Communications Commission (FCC) from 1981 to 1987. He has advised governments and private industry clients on telecommunications ventures and regulatory reforms in Latin America, including in Argentina and Mexico.

Kim Fuad is the London bureau chief for *Petroleum Intelligence Weekly*. A Venezuelan journalist with more than thirty years of experience, he has specialized in reporting on the Latin American oil industry. He has worked for international news agencies, newspapers, and magazines, including Associated Press, United Press International, the *Financial Times*, and *Business Week*.

Pablo L. Gerchunoff is a researcher at the Center for Economic Research at the Instituto Torcuato Di Tella and a consultant for the Economic Commission for Latin America and the Caribbean (ECLAC) on privatization and deregulation. He has worked as a consultant for the Social Enterprise of Energy (ESEDA) for the province of Buenos Aires, and has served as chief of the Cabinet of Assistants for the minister of the economy of Argentina. He holds a degree in economics from the Universidad de Buenos Aires.

Dominique Hachette de la Fresnaye received his degree in economics from the University of Chile and his M.A. and Ph.D. in economics from the University of Chicago. Currently a professor at the Institute of Economics of the Pontificia Universidad Católica de Chile, he is also a consultant for the World Bank and the U.S. Agency for International Development (USAID). He is a coauthor of several books, including *Chile 2010; Liberalizing Foreign Trade: Chile; Desarrollo Económico en Democracia;* and *Financiamiento de la Educación Superior: Antecedentes y Desafíos.* His current research interests are privatization, trade policy, economic integration, and urban development.

Edgar Harrell is the programs and operations director for Price Waterhouse International Privatization Group (IPG). He has a strong private sector background and a number of years of service with the U.S. Agency for International Development (USAID) dedicated to the development of the private sector and advancing privatization programs worldwide. During his career at USAID, he held a number of positions, including special assistant to the USAID administrator for commercialization of technology, deputy assistant administrator of the Bureau for Private Enterprise, and mission director in Jordan. Dr. Harrell holds a Ph.D. in international economics from Columbia University and is a graduate of Harvard's Advanced Management Program.

Rolf J. Lüders is a professor of economics and research program director at the Institute of Economics of the Pontificia Universidad Católica de Chile. He has been, among other positions, dean of the Faculty of Economics and Social Sciences at Catholic University (1968–1971), director of the Capital Market Development Program of the Organization of American States (1971–1974), member of one of the legislative commissions (1974–1981), and secretary of trade and secretary of finance (1982–1983). He has coauthored several books and numerous journal articles. Today, besides his academic activities, he does occasional consulting for several institutions, among them the World Bank and the United Nations, and is chief economist of the International Center for Economic Growth.

Joseph A. Mann, Jr., is the Venezuelan correspondent for the *Financial Times* of London and the publisher of a weekly analytical report on Venezuela called *Political Impact.* He has been based in Caracas since 1974 and has worked as a consultant in public relations and political analysis for private companies and for the public sector in Venezuela. In 1982 Mr.

Mann cofounded VenEconomia C.A., a company that edits publications on Venezuelan economic and political themes. A native of Pittsfield, Massachusetts, Mr. Mann obtained his B.S. degree in 1968 from Union College in Schenectady, New York.

William A. Orme, Jr., is a New York–based journalist covering Latin American affairs and a monthly columnist for *América Economía*, a Latin American business magazine. One of his current projects includes researching and writing a book on the U.S.-Mexico free trade agreement for a new *Washington Post* "Briefing Book" series. He was the founding editor of *LatinFinance* magazine and held that position from 1988 to 1991. From 1981 to 1988 Mr. Orme lived in Mexico City, where he worked as a correspondent for various publications and news services, including *The Washington Post, The Economist, The Journal of Commerce,* and *The Financial Times.* He earned his B.A. in Latin American Studies from Friends World College in Huntington, New York.

Ben Petrazzini is a doctoral candidate in the Department of Communication at the University of California, San Diego. He has done extensive research on privatization, especially in the telecommunications industry. He holds a law degree from the Universidad Nacional de Córdoba in Argentina, a master's degree in social science from the Facultad Latinoamericana de Ciencias Sociales in Buenos Aires, and a master's degree in sociology from the Universidad Católica Argentina. He has served as an advisor in Argentina's national Camara de Diputados.

Peter Phillips is a cabinet minister without portfolio in the Office of the Prime Minister of Jamaica. He was educated at Jamaica College and later studied at the University of the West Indies, where he received his bachelor's degree and master's degree in economics and government, and at the State University of New York, where he received his doctorate in political economy and development studies.

Aileen Amarandos Pisciotta is international communications counsel at Latham & Watkins, based in Washington, D.C. The Latham & Watkins Communications Group has advised companies and governments in Europe, Latin America, Asia, and the Pacific Rim with respect to transactions and regulatory changes concerning telecommunications liberalization and privatization. Ms. Pisciotta was special assistant to the chief of the U.S. Federal Communications Commission Common Carrier Bureau (1982–1983) and has been cochairman of the American Bar Assocation International Section Communications Committee since 1989. She has advised governments and private industry clients on telecommunications ventures, privatizations, and regulatory reforms in Latin America, including in Argentina, Ecuador, Mexico, Nicaragua, and Venezuela.

Carlos A. Primo Braga   is an economist in the International Trade Division of the World Bank. Before joining the World Bank, Dr. Primo Braga was an assistant professor of economics at the University of São Paulo and a senior researcher at the Fundação Instituto de Pesquisas Econômicas in São Paulo, Brazil. He has also served as an economic consultant to many private companies, multilateral agencies, and government institutions in Brazil and abroad. Since 1988, he has been a visiting professor at the Johns Hopkins School of Advanced International Studies in Washington, D.C. Dr. Primo Braga holds a bachelor's degree in mechanical engineering and a master's degree in economics from the University of São Paulo and a Ph.D. in economics from the University of Illinois at Urbana-Champaign. The views expressed in his paper are his alone and should not be attributed to the World Bank, its Board of Directors, its management, or any of its member countries.

Ravi Ramamurti   is the Joseph Riesman Associate Professor of Business Administration at Northeastern University in Boston. He obtained his doctorate in business administration from Harvard Business School, where he was also a visiting professor in the business, government, and competition area from 1986 to 1988. He has done research on the management, control, and privatization of state-owned enterprises for more than fifteen years. He has worked in the state enterprise sector and in government and has served as a consultant to several developing countries and international agencies.

Rogelio Ramírez de la O   is president of Ecanal, a private research company that publishes *Economic Report on Mexico* and *Special Report on Mexico*, in which Dr. Ramírez analyzes economic trends, prospects, and government policy in Mexico. Ecanal's clientele consists mainly of large multinational corporations with investments and interests in Mexico. Dr. Ramírez has published extensively on the macroeconomy and on international trade and investment. He has written a book on foreign investment policy in Mexico and contributed to U.S. academic journals and to books on Mexico's foreign debt, the privatization of state enterprises, the impact of the North American Free Trade Agreement, and the economic outlook in Mexico. He holds a Ph.D. in economics from Cambridge University and a bachelor's degree in economics from the National Autonomous University of Mexico.

James B. Sullivan   is director of the Office of Energy and Infrastructure, Bureau for Research and Development, U.S. Agency for International Development (USAID). Dr. Sullivan joined USAID in 1982 as an energy consultant in Pakistan and has served in his present capacity since 1986. Previously he was with the U.S. Environmental Protection Agency and the U.S. Office of Technology Assessment, continuing to work with innovative energy technologies, economic development, and environmental quality. Dr. Sullivan founded the Center for Science in the Public Interest and served as its codirector from 1970 to 1976, directing projects on a variety of energy and environmental issues. Dr. Sullivan graduated from Manhattan College with a degree in civil engineering. He holds a master's degree from New York University and a doctorate from the Massachusetts Institute of Technology in applied mathematics and hydrodynamics.

INDEX

ICEG Academic Advisory Board